DISABILITY INSURANCE AND PUBLIC POLICY

SAMUEL A. REA, jr

Disability Insurance and Public Policy

PUBLISHED FOR THE ONTARIO ECONOMIC COUNCIL BY
UNIVERSITY OF TORONTO PRESS
TORONTO BUFFALO LONDON

© Ontario Economic Council 1981
Printed in Canada
Reprinted in 2018
ISBN 0-8020-3383-0
ISBN 978-1-4875-7323-2 (paper)

Canadian Cataloguing in Publication Data

Rea, Samuel A., 1944-
  Disability insurance and public policy
  Bibliography: p.
  ISBN 0-8020-3383-0
  1. Insurance, Disability – Canada. 2. Canada – Social Policy.
  I. Ontario Economic Council. II. Title.
  HD7106.C2R42   368.4'1'00971   C81-094673-4

This report reflects the views of the author and not necessarily those of the Ontario Economic Council or the Ontario government. The Council establishes policy questions to be investigated and commissions research projects, but it does not influence the conclusions or recommendations of authors. The decision to sponsor publication of this study was based on its competence and relevance to public policy and was made with the advice of anonymous referees expert in the area.

Contents

ACKNOWLEDGMENTS vii

1
Introduction 3

2
The market for safety and insurance 9

3
The uneasy case for mandatory disability insurance 25

4
Disability benefits 39

5
Administrative issues 77

6
Evaluation of existing programs 92

7
Conclusions 108

APPENDICES

A Adverse selection and mandatory insurance 115
B Income-tested government programs and mandatory insurance 121

BIBLIOGRAPHY 133

Acknowledgments

I wish to thank Yehuda Kotowitz, Charles Wilson, Michael Mendelson, and two anonymous referees for their helpful comments. The Canadian Association of Accident and Sickness Insurers, James Clare, and John H. Miller provided useful information. Mary Crossan deserves special thanks for typing and retyping the manuscript. The author, of course, assumes responsibility for the views expressed.

DISABILITY INSURANCE AND PUBLIC POLICY

1
Introduction

Without some form of outside assistance, victims of accident or illness are likely to suffer economic hardship. Clearly some form of insurance against disability is desirable, whether publicly or privately provided. Numerous government programs such as workmen's compensation and public pension plans partially compensate some of those who are disabled. Courts award compensation under common law in accident cases involving negligence. Furthermore, laws and regulations govern the performance of potentially risky activities in order to reduce the number of accidents.

However, the fact that criticism of the existing system is widespread suggests that the existing collection of government programs is not efficient at either insuring citizens against disability or encouraging optimal precautions against accidents. Virtually all the current programs are under attack. Workmen's compensation benefits are considered inadequate by the disabled and too costly by industry spokesmen. Governments in Manitoba and Saskatchewan have suggested that workmen's compensation be extended to non-work accidents. In the United States a doubling of the incidence of disability under the Social Security Program has brought the program under close scrutiny.

The greatest changes in the existing system are now occurring in the courts. In the absence of alternative means of compensating accident victims, the courts seem to be relaxing the negligence standard in order to compensate all accident victims. Although the relatively conservative Canadian courts have lagged behind those in the United States, the trend is inevitable because of growing concern for accident victims. In 1977 a Vermont court awarded a skier $1.5 million in damages because the operators of a ski area failed to close or adequately groom a ski trail. The decision implied that owners of ski areas could be liable for most accidents on their hills. In response to this case the Vermont Legislature later passed a law which forces Vermont courts to return to the criterion for awarding

4 Disability insurance and public policy

compensation that prevailed prior to the 1977 decision.[1] The earlier doctrine held that a skier assumes the inherent risk of skiing and thus cannot collect from the ski operator for accidents which result from that risk. This case and many others show that the common law is an extremely inefficient mechanism for compensating accident victims. The problems associated with court-determined compensation have resulted in the introduction of no-fault automobile insurance in Quebec. A committee of the Ontario government has recently recommended that no-fault automobile insurance be introduced in Ontario. The no-fault approach is not new. Ontario eliminated the employee's right to sue his employer when workmen's compensation was introduced in 1915.

There is also increasing pressure for producers of consumer products to compensate consumers who suffer accidents while using those products. Although Canada has not followed the United States in eliminating the negligence test (and substituting strict liability) Canadian decisions employ a standard that is close to strict liability (Fleming 1977, 508; Linden 1977, 495). If such a change does not occur through court decisions, it is likely to be brought about through legislation. The Saskatchewan Consumer Products Warranties Act, 1977, makes the manufacturer or seller liable for damages caused by defective products and places the onus of proof on the manufacturer to demonstrate that the product was not defective. Furthermore, government legislation of the safety of consumer products is likely to become increasingly strict.

The forms of insurance and compensation for disability now existing in Canada are unco-ordinated, and they are not evolving together. The distinction between accidents to consumers, automobile drivers, or workers is misleading; a potential accident victim requires insurance against disability regardless of where and how an accident might occur. Yet Canadians are financing a growing variety of overlapping disability schemes. The resulting combination of programs is likely to be an extremely inefficient way of providing insurance coverage.

Current coverage can also be irrational. A worker who is permanently disabled because of an on-the-job accident can collect tax-free workmen's compensation, a Canada Pension Plan (CPP) disability pension, and private disability insurance. If he is injured in an automobile accident as a result of someone else's negligence, he can collect full compensation (including 'pain and suffering') through a successful tort action, along with a Canada Pension Plan disability pension and possibly private insurance. In contrast, if his (non-working) wife is

1 *Vermont Statutes Annotated*, Title 12, Chapter 61, 1037: 'A person who takes part in any sport accepts as a matter of law the dangers that inhere therein insofar as they are obvious and necessary.' The law came into effect on 7 February 1978; New Hampshire passed a similar law the same year.

Introduction 5

permanently disabled as a result of a fall in the home, she will receive nothing to offset her loss of ability to earn income in the future or the cost of hiring someone to assist her in taking care of the household, let alone 'pain and suffering.'

There have been a few studies of overall compensation systems. In New Zealand the Woodhouse Report (New Zealand, 1967) led to the introduction of a government-run insurance program for all accidents regardless of fault; the right to claim damages under common law was eliminated. Studies in Manitoba (1977) and Saskatchewan (1976) have suggested that these two provinces should consider following New Zealand's example. These two provincial reports are deficient because they give little consideration to the economic issues involved in the design of such a far-reaching program.

A common deficiency of many of the previous studies is that they fail to recognize that the programs that provide income to those who are disabled, including welfare programs, can all be thought of as insurance schemes. In other words the existence of the programs implies that a member of society has a claim on the other members of society should he become disabled. This claim reduces the risk of income fluctuation that each member of society faces and raises everyone's expected utility. When the programs are viewed as insurance, it becomes possible to determine the level of benefits that will make members of society better off before they know who will be disabled. The optimal amount of insurance can be derived by analysing the tradeoff between the reduced income (because of payment of premiums) in the event that there is no disability and the income that is received as insurance benefits if a disability occurs. When the benefits of compensation to the disabled are compared to the cost of premiums to all the insured, it can be seen that it is just as bad to have too much insurance as too little.

If a program that provides income for the disabled is viewed as insurance, its redistributive effects must be analysed before it is known who will be disabled. Such a program will raise the expected utility of some groups more than that of others. The patterns of redistribution will probably differ widely. For instance, workmen's compensation is unlikely to shift income from capital to labour; its most likely effect would be redistribution from low-risk to high-risk workers, from risk-loving workers (those willing to accept a lower expected return to increase risk) to risk-averse workers (those willing to accept a lower expected return to reduce risk), and from owners of safer firms to owners of risky firms. In the consumer context a decision to award $1.5 million to an injured skier does not help injured skiers at the expense of ski areas. Instead, it raises the price of skiing for all consumers. Within the group of consumers, it raises the welfare of bad skiers at the expense of good skiers and risk-averse skiers at the expense

6 Disability insurance and public policy

of risk-loving skiers. The reduction in rents earned by ski areas is likely to be small in comparison to the redistribution between groups of skiers.

Furthermore, analyses of disability compensation have not considered the relationship between insurance and safety. Policies that affect insurance will also affect decisions concerning safety precautions. For example, take flood hazards. The U.S. government was not satisfied that homeowners were making rational decisions with respect to insurance against losses due to floods. This lack of interest in insurance may have been caused in part by the availability of what amounted to insurance in the form of government aid to those in flooded areas. Flood insurance was made mandatory in areas subject to flood damage for those wishing to receive government-guaranteed mortgages. This coverage in turn reduced private incentives to locate away from the most flood-prone areas and to build houses that would minimize losses. Additional regulations were therefore introduced to prevent construction in the most frequently flooded areas and to specify construction methods.

The same connection between safety and insurance occurs in the context of disability. Safety refers to the probability that there will be no disability. Precautions can be taken that will reduce the frequency and severity of disability. In the case of occupational health and safety, the existence of the workmen's compensation system will tend to lessen the precautions taken by employers and employees. In the case of automobile accidents, a change from a system of fault-based liability coupled with third-party liability insurance to a system of no-fault personal injury insurance will tend to influence the frequency and severity of automobile accidents. In other words, an adequate analysis of disability insurance must consider the degree to which the safety precautions taken by economic agents will be affected.

Most government policies on insurance and safety are based on the idea that the market would not provide an appropriate amount of insurance and safety without government intervention. In principle that idea is incorrect. Chapter 2 presents a basic economic model that shows the optimal amount of insurance and safety precautions that should be taken. The analysis emphasizes that it is efficient to invest resources in preventing accidents until the marginal cost of avoiding accidents equals the marginal cost of the accidents. The cost of accidents will reflect the society's lost production and the individual's lost utility or 'pain and suffering.' In practical terms we want to guarantee that producers invest the appropriate amount in the design of safer products, that production processes are rearranged to minimize the cost of on-the-job accidents and occupational illness, and that consumers buy products and services based on the risk of accidents in both the production of them and their consumption. Chapter 2 shows how a perfectly functioning market would provide the optimal amount of insurance and safety in the workplace in the absence of government intervention of any kind.

A crucial feature of insurance markets is imperfect information. For example, a buyer of insurance may not know accurately what risks he will face, and the insurance company is unsure whether an individual is a particularly bad risk. Imperfect information can take a number of forms, all of which affect the market's ability to provide the optimal insurance and safety. Throughout this book, therefore, the importance of imperfect information will be emphasized. In Chapter 2 the effect of moral hazard (the ability of an insurance carrier to monitor the insured person's precautions) on the market level of insurance is analysed.

The most important policy issue concerning disability is whether disability insurance should be mandatory or voluntary.[2] Most current government policies, such as strict liability of producers for consumer injuries, Workmen's Compensation, and no-fault insurance, are essentially forms of mandatory insurance. There would be no reason to have mandatory insurance if the market could provide the optimal insurance. Mandatory insurance is justified only if the market does not provide enough insurance *and* if the government can improve the situation. Two general characteristics of disability insurance make it likely that the market will provide the wrong amount of safety or insurance, imperfect information and externalities. However, making disability insurance mandatory will not necessarily improve the level of safety or insurance. The analysis in Chapter 3 shows that the case for mandatory coverage is not very persuasive.

The insurance market model and the analysis of imperfect information developed in Chapters 2 and 3 is used in Chapter 4 to analyse the design of public and private disability benefits. The analysis sheds light on such important issues as the measurement of partial disability, the indexation of benefits, and the taxation of disability benefits. The integration of disability programs is also considered, because as long as more than one program provides disability benefits there must be a way of co-ordinating the different systems to avoid overcompensation, undercompensation, and excessive administrative costs.

Another issue dealt with in Chapter 4 is the choice between lump-sum and periodic payments as compensation for disability. Courts award lump-sum compensation if the defendant is found liable for a disability, but most insurance programs such as Workmen's Compensation and private insurance benefits

---

2 This issue is analytically distinct from the choice between public and private insurance carriers.

provide periodic payments. The courts have suggested that periodic payment may be a more appropriate form of compensation.[3] Chapter 4 shows, however, that the case for lump-sum benefits is much stronger than is generally appreciated.

An important consideration in formulating policies towards disability is that an adequate program is bound to entail high administrative costs arising primarily from imperfect information. Administrative resources must be devoted to monitoring precautions, discovering the causes of accidents, and determining the extent of disability. As a result, any system must invariably compromise between providing optimal insurance to a population on the one hand and on the other avoiding and minimizing accidents and administrative costs. Chapter 5 deals with administrative issues, such as the design of a process for determining if a disability has occurred and the measurement of fault for programs that assign the cost of accidents to those responsible. Administrative costs are a central factor in the choice between a fault-based tort law and no-fault system in which each person is required to insure himself against his own disability. The no-fault controversy is also analysed in that chapter.

Chapter 5 considers as well a number of other controversial issues that hinge on administrative efficiency. For example, a system may have either separate insurance programs for specific groups, such as Workmen's Compensation for workers, or a universal program. A single universal program may provide substantial savings in administrative costs but can introduce other inefficiencies. The chapter also discusses the choice between public and private provision of insurance and examines the criticism that insurance risk classifications are discriminatory. The last two chapters analyse the existing programs in Canada and Ontario in light of the analytical framework developed in Chapters 2 through 5 and discuss alternatives to the current system.

This study does not include any new empirical information on the operation of disability insurance systems. Rather, it is intended to provide a theoretical framework for the analysis of disability insurance. Except for Chapter 6, it is applicable to countries other than Canada. Much of the analysis can also be directly applied to other social insurance programs and should be of interest to anyone studying insurance markets and alternatives to tort compensation.

---

3 *Andrews* v. *Grand & Toy Alberta Ltd.*, [1978] S.C.R. 229, at 236

2
The market for safety and insurance

INTRODUCTION

Many people believe that government policies that impose mandatory insurance and safety are a good thing. That is not necessarily true. Under certain circumstances the market alone will provide the optimal amount of insurance and safety without government intervention. In such cases government intervention can only make the public worse off. This chapter outlines a model of how the level of voluntary insurance would be determined by the market alone. The model shows that policies towards disability insurance must consider the effects of such programs on the level of safety, because the decision to insure against income loss is made simultaneously with, and balanced against, the decision to take preventive measures, or precautions, that reduce the chance of a disability occurring.

First we look at the decision to purchase insurance with the probability of disability assumed constant. Next we look at the decision to take safety precautions without insurance. Then the simultaneous decision to purchase insurance and safety is examined, and we see that as long as the insurance premium reflects the precautions actually taken, individuals will choose the optimal amount of insurance and safety.

Many of the decisions on insurance and safety are in reality expressed indirectly when employees choose jobs based on working conditions and fringe benefits or when consumers choose products based on product safety and guarantees. The labour market is therefore examined, and it is found that such indirect methods of choosing insurance and safety can still provide the optimal amount of both. The implications of the model for the observed relationship between wages and safety are then analysed.

10 Disability insurance and public policy

The analysis up to that point assumes that everyone has access to perfect information. Risks and costs are known accurately to all parties. The next question arises when imperfect information is brought into the model, as it is in reality. The final section therefore discusses how imperfect information creates the problem of moral hazard and alters both the insurance contract and the amount of safety that would be provided by the free action of the market.

The next chapter will use this framework to see whether other imperfections in the market besides those considered in this chapter justify government intervention in the form of mandatory disability insurance.

THE DECISION TO PURCHASE INSURANCE

Consumers and workers face risks in their daily activities. These hazards may lead to loss of property or loss of ability to earn income. There may also be loss of enjoyment of life because of injury or sickness. To some extent individuals can insure themselves against these losses by finding some institution that is willing to bear the risk. An insurance company makes itself able to assume an individual's risk by selling insurance to many persons, most of whom will never make a claim.

The decision to purchase insurance is just like any consumption decision (see Ehrlich and Becker 1972). The only difference is that the insurance decision involves a choice between the amounts of utility the consumer would have under each possible outcome. These alternative outcomes, corresponding to different amounts of loss, are called 'states of the world.' The kinds and amounts of insurance purchased reflect the consumer's desires and expectations. In the simplest case, where someone faces the risk of a decline in income but no disability or other loss, the decision is straightforward. If the price of insurance accurately reflects the probability of the occurrence and amount of loss, the risk-averse individual will fully insure. This means that no matter what happens he will end up with the same income (which would be lower than if he paid no premiums and never had an accident).

In the case where there is a risk of non-pecuniary loss, perhaps caused by personal injury, the decision is more complicated (see Mathematical note 1). The 'pain and suffering" will not be insured against because additional consumption in the event of injury will be worth less than the consumption given up in the form of an insurance premium. The optimal insurance principle suggests that rational consumers will not insure against nonmonetary losses as long as the marginal utility of income is not affected by the injury.

The optimal amount of insurance will depend, among other things, on the type of injury. Someone in a coma will not have any use for income as long as

Mathematical note 1
The decision to purchase insurance

Consider someone with utility equal to $U(C_0)$ in the event that there is no injury, C_0 being consumption if there is no injury. Should there be an injury, utility equals $V(C_1)$. For the moment the probability of injury is assumed fixed. For simplicity only one time period is considered, and it is assumed that an injury reduces income to zero. Consumption can only be maintained if insurance is purchased. The individual chooses the level of insurance to maximize his expected utility:

$$U^* = aU(w - g) + (1 - a)V(m(g) - g), \tag{1}$$

where a is the probability that there is no injury, w is the wage income, g is the insurance premium, $m(g)$ is the insurance benefit (gross of the premium), and $U' > 0$, $U'' < 0$, $V' > 0$, $V'' < 0$. Note that the premium is paid whether one is healthy or disabled, but ut the benefit is only paid if one is disabled. Ehrlich and Becker (1972) define the benefit to be net of the premium.

If utility is maximized with respect to g, the first-order conditions require that

$$-aU' + (1 - a)V'(m' - 1) = 0, \tag{2}$$

or

$$U'/V' = [(1 - a)/a](m' - 1). \tag{3}$$

The first-order condition implies that the marginal utility of consumption in each of the two states of the world must equal the 'price' at which income can be transferred between these two states. This is analogous to equating the marginal rate of substitution between two goods to the price ratio in a more typical consumption decision. If the insurance is actuarially fair and there are no costs of administering the insurance, the insurance premium depends only on the probability

$$m(g) = g/(1 - a), \tag{4}$$

$$m' = 1/(1 - a), \text{ and}$$

$$U' = V'. \tag{5}$$

The consumer will purchase insurance until the marginal utility of consumption is equalized between the two states of the world. There is no way to improve the position of the consumer by shifting consumption between the two states. In other words the level of insurance is optimal.

If the accident does not alter the utility that is derived from consumption, $U' = V'$ when $C_0 = C_1$. Given this utility function, insurance will cover all pecuniary losses. Notice that this does not imply that $U(C_0) = V(C_0)$. Since an injured person will experience a loss of utility, it follows that $U(C_0) > V(C_0)$.

12 Disability insurance and public policy

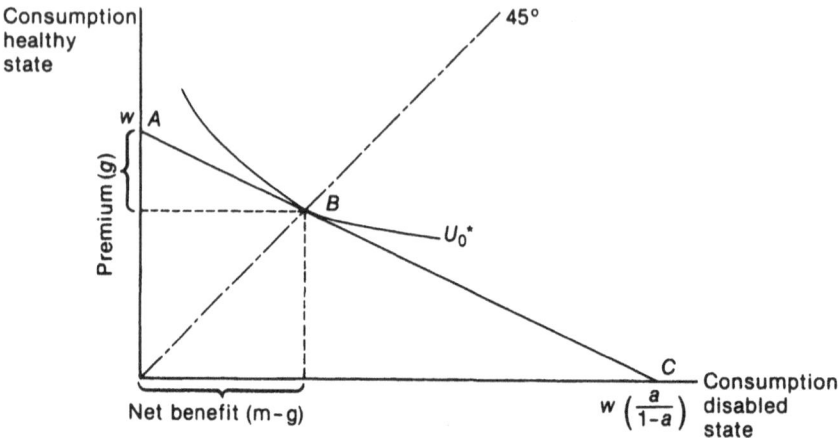

Figure 1: The insurance decision. In Ehrlich and Becker's (1972) exposition of the insurance decision, the budget constraint is ABC, with a slope equal to $-[a/(1-a)]$. For every dollar of consumption in the healthy state, $a/(1-a)$ dollars of consumption in the disabled state can be obtained. The indifference curve U_0^* represents the rate at which the individual is willing to trade off consumption in the two states of the world, which depends on the probability of each state occurring and on the utility function in each state. Utility is maximized with equal amounts of consumption, but not utility, in both states of the world. This result occurs if $U'(X) = V'(X)$.

his medical expenses are paid for (and he has no dependants). Other injuries may lead to more goods-intensive as opposed to time-intensive consumption (Becker 1965). This would make greater insurance coverage optimal ($C_1 > C_0$ when $U' = V'$).

The optimal insurance model casts some light on common law compensation. The tort victim is entitled to sufficient compensation to 'place the victim in the same position he was in before the accident occurred' (Charles 1977, 39). The model indicates that if tort compensation is viewed as insurance paid for by the victim, the level of compensation is too high. (In the economic model the tort compensation would be an amount A such that $U(w) = V(A)$. In most cases this will be an amount that greatly exceeds earnings because $U(w) > V(w)$. The difference between w and A is the non-pecuniary loss, a portion of which is often called 'pain and suffering.') This point is discussed further in Chapter 6.

Mathematical note 2
The decision to purchase safety

Precautions are assumed to be taken regardless of whether one turns out to be healthy or disabled, an assumption that simplifies the discussion but does not significantly alter the results. Assume that income falls from w to m in the event of disability but that there is no insurance. The individual will vary his precautions and expenditures on safety so as to maximize expected utility:

$$U^* = a(d, q)U(C_0, d) + [1 - a(d, q)]V(C_1, d), \tag{6}$$

subject to $C_0 = w - q$ and $C_1 = m$, where C_0 is consumption in the healthy state, C_1 is consumption in the disabled state, d is precautions taken by the individual, and q is expenditures on safety, $a_q > 0, a_{qq} < 0$. Substitution gives $U^* = a(d, q)U(w - q, d) + [1 - a(d, q)]V(m - q, d)$. The first-order conditions are as follows:

$$\partial U^*/\partial d = a_d(U - V) + aU_d + (1 - a)V_d = 0,$$

or

$$a_d(U - V) = -[aU_d + (1 - a)V_d], \tag{7}$$

$$\partial U^*/\partial q = a_q(U - V) - aU_C - (1 - a)V_C = 0,$$

or

$$a_q(U - V) = aU_C + (1 - a)V_C. \tag{8}$$

THE DECISION TO PURCHASE SAFETY

In reality the probability of an accident that produces disability is not constant but depends in part on how much safety the individual is willing to buy. The level of safety can be increased in two ways: first, income can be diverted from consumption to the purchase of safety. This might be in the form of a safety device, a higher quality consumer product (which costs more), or a safer job (which offers a lower wage). Second, the individual might take precautions that lower the risk of accidents but are inconvenient and therefore costly in terms of forgone utility.

The safety decision can be illustrated in a simple one-period model similar to the insurance model (see Mathematical note 2). Precautions will be taken until the expected disutility of precautions in absolute value equals the marginal

14 Disability insurance and public policy

reduction in expected utility. Similarly expenditures will be made until the expected marginal utility of income equals the marginal reduction in expected utility. Both conditions make it clear that the costs of safety must be weighed against the benefits of safety. If safety were costless, there would be no limit on the optimal amount of safety.

THE RELATIONSHIP BETWEEN SAFETY AND INSURANCE

The existence of insurance lowers the returns to safety precautions and raises the probability of disability. To overcome this disincentive to take precautions, the seller of insurance must make the insurance premium reflect the actual probability of an accident. That means, the seller of insurance must know the level of precautions taken by the individual and his expenditures on safety. Although he is insured, the individual will purchase an efficient amount of safety because reduced precautions will increase his insurance premiums. If taking precautions does not lower the premium, the problem of moral hazard arises; it is examined later in this chapter.

Mathematical note 3 shows that when the premium reflects the level of safety precautions and expenditures, still assuming perfect information, the individual will invest in an efficient amount of safety. We can conclude that the safety decision is not affected by the availability of insurance as long as the insurance company can costlessly monitor the precautions and expenditures on safety. The consequences of imperfect information, including the inability of an insurance carrier to monitor precautions, will be considered below.

OCCUPATIONAL SAFETY AND INSURANCE

One could argue that the most important decisions an individual makes concerning safety and insurance are made in conjunction with other transactions. For instance, when consumers buy consumer products they may vary the level of safety by varying the quality or type of good consumed, as well as by altering the precautions taken when using the product. The products may come with guarantees or warranties that serve as insurance policies. The manufacturer's liability (under common law or consumer protection statutes) for damages resulting from product failure also provide insurance protection for the consumer.

The choice of employer or occupation can also be tied in with a decision concerning safety and insurance. Different types of employment differ not only in inherent risk but also in the safety precautions that employees are expected to take and the disability insurance benefits available to workers. The employment model will be introduced in this section and used in the next chapter to analyse

Mathematical note 3
The purchase of safety and insurance with perfect information

When safety is endogenous, the individual will maximize expected utility by choosing m, q, and d:

$$U^* = a(d,q)U(w - g(m,d,q) - q, d) + [1 - a(d,q)]V(m - g(m,d,q) - q, d). \quad (9)$$

The first-order conditions are as follows:

$$\partial U^*/\partial m = aU_c(-g_m) + (1-a)V_c(1-g_m) = 0, \quad (10)$$

$$\partial U^*/\partial q = a_q(U-V) + aU_c(-g_q - 1) + (1-a)V_c(-g_q - 1) = 0, \quad (11)$$

$$\partial U^*/\partial d = a_d(U-V) + aU_d + (1-a)V_d - aU_c g_d - (1-a)V_c g_d = 0. \quad (12)$$

If the insurance carrier has no costs and can costlessly determine the level of precautions and expenditures, the premium g will equal $(1 - a(d,q))m$ and the individual will take into account the effect of his actions on the premium. Therefore $g_m = 1 - a$, $g_d = -a_d m$, and $g_q = -a_q m$. Equation (10) reduces to $U_c = V_c$ as before, and equation (11) becomes

$$a_q(U - V + mU_c) = U_c. \quad (11a)$$

In other words there is an investment in safety until the marginal utility of income equals the marginal increase in expected utility. The latter consists of the uncompensated loss of utility $(U - V)$ and the insured loss of utility mU_c. Equation (12) reduces to

$$a_d[U - V + mU_c] = -[aU_d + (1-a)V_d], \quad (12a)$$

with a similar interpretation.

---

mandatory disability insurance, such as workmen's compensation. The basic structure of the model can also be applied to the choice of consumer products (Spence 1977).

In choosing an employer, a worker will consider all aspects of the job, such as wages, fringe benefits, and working conditions. He will seek employment that provides the combination of job characteristics that maximizes his utility. Conversely, the employer will alter compensation and working conditions so as to maximize the worker's utility at a given cost. Regardless of whether or not the employer is a monopsonist, for any given cost he will wish to choose the job characteristics that attract employees. Naturally the employer also wishes to lower the total cost, but for the purposes of this study we are interested in the compensation package that will be offered to workers. The compensation package includes the wage, a disability benefit, a level of precautions taken by the firm, and a level of precautions expected of the worker. The optimal levels of safety and insurance for an industry with homogeneous workers and firms are derived in Mathematical note 4.

It can easily be shown that competition between firms and the expected utility-maximizing behaviour of workers will provide the optimal amount of insurance and safety without government intervention provided there is perfect information. If the firm is the only employer in an area (a monopsonist) it may use too little labour in order to keep wages low, but, given the amount of labour used, the level of safety will be efficient. The monopsonist, like the competitive firm, has an incentive to offer the package of working conditions that maximizes worker utility for a given cost to the firm.[1]

The efficiency of the market outcome, however, only holds if there is perfect information and there are no externalities. When imperfect information is introduced, the equilibrium disability benefits and safety will be altered, as we shall see.

RISK-COMPENSATING WAGE DIFFERENTIALS

We have seen that firms have an incentive to provide safety because it allows them to pay lower wages. The existence of different wages for different risks, called compensating wage differentials, would support the theory. If there were no compensating wage differentials, that would mean either that the market is affected (as we know it is) by imperfect information and externalities or that our reasoning is wrong.

The argument above assumed that workers were homogeneous within a given labour market and that there was no movement between labour markets. It assumed too that all firms had the same production function. No risk-related wage differential could exist because all workers received the same wage; it was the threat of having to increase wages to keep workers that induced firms to offer an efficient amount of job safety. In real life workers have different attitudes to risk and firms spend different amounts on safety. These differences will now be introduced into the model. We examine first the case in which workers are identical and firms differ in their costs of accident avoidance (Mathematical note 5). Then we consider the general case in which both workers and firms differ (Mathematical note 6). Perfect information is still assumed. In light of these arguments we consider the empirical data available on risk differentials.

Empirical evidence on risk differentials
The theoretical discussion indicates that empirical studies of wage differentials may not provide an adequate test of the economic model or show whether

---

1 This holds if workers are homogeneous. If the marginal worker is less risk-averse, there will be too little safety.

The market for safety and insurance 17

Mathematical note 4
Optimal levels of safety and insurance for an industry with homogeneous workers and firms

Workers are not only interested in wage payments; they are also concerned with payments in the event of disability and with the probability of disability. The probability of disability is reduced by precautions taken by the worker and by the firm, but these precautions are costly to both. The cost to the worker is the additional effort or concentration required for careful work. The employee is assumed to maximize his expected utility, which is a function of the probability of disability, the utility if no disability occurs, and the utility if he is disabled. If the worker is not injured, he receives his wage w, but if he is disabled he receives a disability benefit m. The labour supply is assumed fixed. The expected utility is

$$a(d, s)U(w, d) + [1 - a(d, s)]V(m, d), \qquad (13)$$

where $a(d, s)$ is the probability of no disability, d is the index of worker's safety precautions, s is the index of employer's safety precautions, w is the wage, m is the disability benefit, $U(w, d)$ is the utility if not disabled ($U_w > 0$, $U_{ww} < 0$, $U_d < 0$, $U_{dd} < 0$), $V(m, d)$ is the utility if disabled ($V_m > 0$, $V_{mm} < 0$, $V_d < 0$, $V_{dd} < 0$), and $U > V$ if $w = m$.

Safety precautions can enter the firm's profit equation in at least four ways. First, they affect the supply of labour to the firm and the wage and benefit package that is offered. Second, they impose costs that may be associated with each job slot. Protective clothing would be the most straightforward example of this type of precaution. Third, the precautions may be associated with capital, i.e. a protective device on a machine. Fourth, the precautions may enter the production function directly. For instance, a lower operating speed will reduce output but will lower the probability of an accident. To simplify the analysis it is assumed that labour is the only factor in the production function. Following Diamond (1977) precautions are assumed to affect the fixed cost of hiring an employee, but the costs per employee are invariant to the level of employment.

Firms will compete for labour by varying the components of the compensation package, broadly defined to include the firm's safety precautions s and the level of employee precautions required d, in addition to the wage w and the disability benefit m. It is assumed that the number of employees in the industry is predetermined. The firm hires workers knowing that some proportion of the workers will become disabled and will be non-productive. Workers are assumed to have homogeneous preferences and productivity. Workers are not paid a wage if they become disabled, but the firm will have to pay disability benefits and will have other costs associated with the disabled worker's job slot. These costs include any specific investment in human capital. Entry of firms into the industry and competition for employees (which causes w, m, d, and s to vary) will guarantee that the expected marginal product of labour equals the expected marginal cost:

$$a(d, s)Z(a) = a(d, s)w + (1 - a(d, s))m + C(s)$$

or (14)

$$Z(a) = w + \frac{1 - a(d, s)}{a(d, s)} m + \frac{C(s)}{a(d, s)},$$

where $Z(a)$ is the marginal revenue product of labour ($Z' < 0$) and $C(s)$ are the fixed costs per worker employed ($C'(s) > 0$, $C''(s) > 0$). The marginal revenue product of labour

18 Disability insurance and public policy

increases as the risk level rises because lower levels of safety reduce the number of employees who actually produce.

The socially optimal level of disability benefits and safety can be determined by maximizing the expected utility of each worker U^* with respect to m, d, and s subject to equation (14):

$$U^* = a(d,s)U\left\{[Z(a) - ((1-a)/a)m - C/a], d\right\} + [1 - a(d,s)]V(m,d). \quad (15)$$

The first-order conditions are as follows:

$$\partial U^*/\partial m = U_w - V_m = 0,$$

or

$$U_w = V_m, \quad (16)$$

$$\partial U^*/\partial d = [aU_d + (1-a)V_d] + a_d[U - V] + [a_d(m + C)U_w]/a + aU_w Z'a_d,$$

or

$$-[aU_d + (1-a)V_d] = a_d[U-V] + a_d[(m+C)/a]U_w + aU_w Z'a_d, \quad (17)$$

$$\partial U^*/\partial s = a_s(U - V)/U_w + a_s(C + m)/a + aZ'a_s - C',$$

or

$$C' = a_s(U-V)/U_w + a_s(C+m)/a + aZ'a_s. \quad (18)$$

The three equations determine the optimal levels of m, d, and s. Equation (16) represents the condition for optimal insurance, given d and s. The marginal utilities are equated between both states of the world. The optimal level of precautions taken by the individual (equation 17) should be such that the expected marginal disutility of the precautions equals the marginal reduction in the compensated loss plus a term that represents a reduction in the amount of disability compensation, the declining marginal productivity of labour, and the cost to the firm of the job slot. The last two terms reflect the greater wage that could be paid if the job is made less hazardous because of worker precautions.

The third condition (equation 18) requires that the firm take safety precautions until the marginal cost of these precautions equals the marginal reduction in uncompensated loss plus the reduction in liability payments, the costs associated with non-productive job slots, and the decline in marginal productivity. $(U - V)/U_w$ represents the wage workers are willing to forgo in return for greater safety.

Mathematical note 5
Heterogeneous firms and homogeneous workers
If firms face different costs of accident avoidance, riskier firms will have to compensate workers with increased compensation (Thaler and Rosen 1975, Thaler 1974). This compensation will take the form of added wages and added insurance benefits because it will

The market for safety and insurance 19

always be optimal for the worker to equate the marginal utility of income in both states of the world. When all individuals are alike, the market relationship between safety and wage rates will trace out an indifference curve (Rosen 1974) as shown in Figure 2. Risky industries will offer higher wages and lower safety. As long as insurance is provided, the slope of the market relationship between wages and safety will provide an estimate of the rate at which workers are willing to substitute wages for safety, holding utility constant (many observations would be needed to estimate the *marginal* rate of substitution of wages for safety):

$$(\partial w/\partial a)_{\bar{u}} = (U - V)/U_w. \tag{19}$$

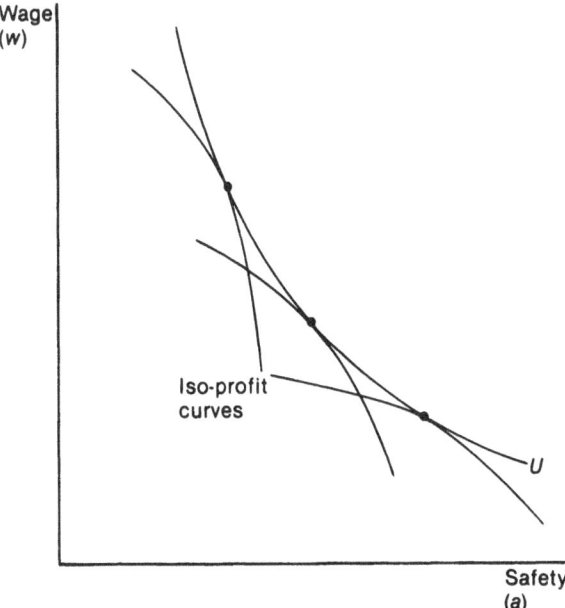

Figure 2: Observed wage differentials, homogeneous workers

This value reflects what the worker would pay in order to lower the probability of injury by a marginal amount, assuming that optimal insurance is provided. If the worker provides his own insurance, Thaler (1974) shows that

$$(\partial w/\partial a)_{\bar{u}} = -[(U - V)/aU_w + m/a^2]. \tag{20}$$

Unfortunately, empirical estimates of $(\partial w/\partial a)_{\bar{u}}$ cannot prove whether or not the market behaves as predicted unless the true value of $(U - V)/U_w$ is known.

Mathematical note 6
Heterogeneous workers and firms

Assume that workers differ in their proneness to accidents and attitudes to risk and that employers can correctly evaluate these differences. If firms face different costs of accident avoidance and employees are heterogeneous, the observed market relationship between wage rates and safety, $w^*(a)$ in Figure 3, will reflect neither the supply nor the demand for safety (Thaler and Rosen 1975). As long as there is mobility between industries or occupations, there are limits on the slope of $w^*(a)$. For instance, a very high compensating differential caused by a large demand for workers in risky jobs would attract some risk-averse or risk-prone workers to riskier industries. $w^*(a)$ could never become steeper than the indifference curves of the most extreme of these workers. Similarly a large number of risk-loving workers could depress the wage premium to the point where the safest firms would find it profitable to use riskier technologies. The slope of $w^*(a)$ would not fall below the wage/safety tradeoff for the safest firm. If enough workers are indifferent to safety, w_a^* would be driven to zero. Firms would still differ in safety because of inherent differences in technology, but the only incentive for safety for the firm would be the lost specific training investment and other costs associated with turnover.

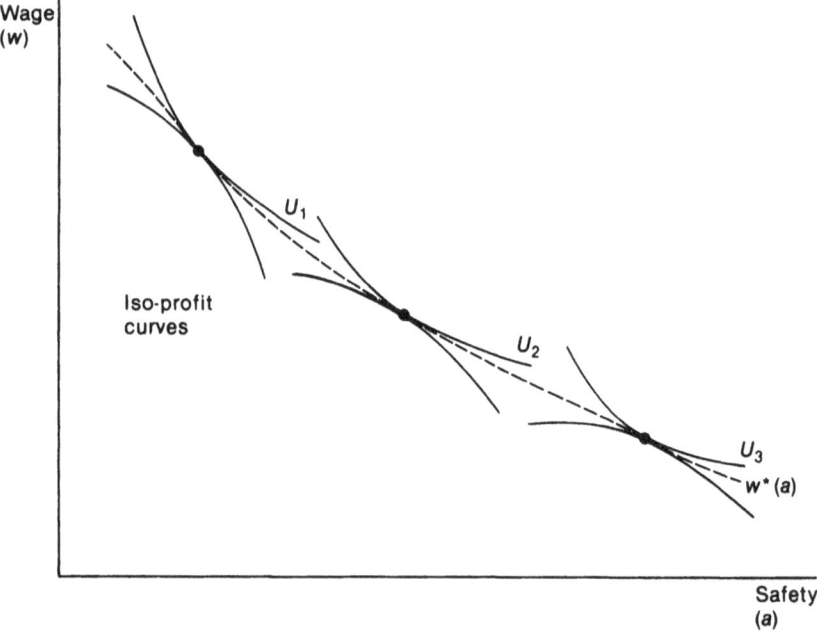

Figure 3: Observed wage differentials, heterogeneous workers and firms

Once mobility between industries is restricted (as in the model used to analyse safety and insurance), the market relationship between wages and safety could take on any shape.

The market for safety and insurance 21

In each market the marginal rate of substitution between wages and safety is implicit but not observed. In Figure 4, there are two separate labour markets, I and II, with higher wage rates and levels of safety in market II. The observed relationship between w and a is positive, but the slopes of the indifference curves and iso-profit curves at I and II are negative. Unfortunately these slopes are unobservable in reality.

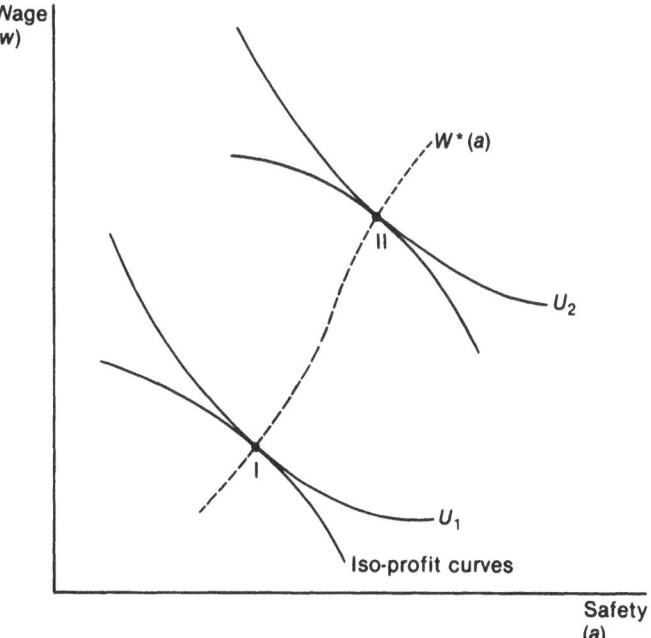

Figure 4: Observed wage differentials, no mobility

workers correctly evaluate risk. There are three basic problems: (1) the difficulty of observing the marginal rate of substitution between wages and safety in each market, (2) the difficulty of determining which groups of workers compete with each other, and (3) the lack of an alternative measure of the value of safety with which to make comparisons.

It is therefore not surprising that economists have only recently attempted to estimate compensating differentials for risk. Smith (1979) summarizes the existing studies. In general, it has been found that although the risk of death has a significant impact on wages, the risk of injury is not consistently important (Smith 1979, 346-7). This absence of support for the model may be caused by measurement problems, by the fact that some of the losses associated with injuries are insured by the employer, or by misperception on the part of workers. The latter is explored in the next chapter.

MORAL HAZARD

So far we have assumed that all parties know accurately what risks they face. However, in reality imperfect information is a crucial problem in insurance markets. Its existence prevents the market from providing the optimal levels of safety and disability insurance. One type of imperfect information is consumers' or workers' lack of accurate knowledge of risk. Another type is the inability of insurance companies (or employers providing benefits) to identify individuals who are accident-prone. This leads to a problem known as adverse selection, which, with the problem of misperception, is analysed in Chapter 3.

Moral hazard arises because of the inability of insurance companies to observe accurately the precautions taken by insured individuals and the size of the loss and it refers to the possibility that the existence of the insurance may induce the insured person to take fewer precautions and exaggerate his losses. For example, the existence of fire insurance on homes may make home owners less careful with fire hazards and may induce them to overstate the extent of any loss or purchase an expensive replacement for a destroyed item. In the context of disability insurance, moral hazard implies that insurance companies cannot easily determine the extent of an injury or its impact on earnings. This type of moral hazard is discussed in relation to benefits in Chapter 4. Our present concern is with the moral hazard that results from the insurance company's inability to monitor the safety precautions taken by those they insure, which makes them unable to reflect risk differentials accurately in their premiums.

We have seen that with perfect information insurance contracts can be structured so that individuals have the incentive to take appropriate precautions. However, when the insured individual's actions cannot be monitored at a reasonable cost, the insurance company will not be able to structure a premium schedule that appropriately rewards safety precautions. Consequently any individual who is fully insured will take too few precautions, so that full insurance will be more expensive than under perfect information. Insurance companies may then find that there is a market for partial insurance, introduced with the use of deductions. Since the partial insurance will induce greater precautions, it is available at a more favourable rate (per dollar of coverage). Buyers may find it preferable to purchase partial insurance in spite of the greater risk it leaves them with. In effect, moral hazard leads to a compromise between two objectives: risk-reduction and provision of safety incentives. If the moral hazard problem is sufficiently great, no insurance will be sold, because each individual will be better off taking precautions and bearing the entire risk than paying a high price for insurance and exercising few precautions.

The irony of moral hazard is that each individual would be made better off if he could demonstrate that he is taking precautions. He cannot do so because the cost of transmitting this information to the insurance company is too high. The reduction in coverage is not always the most economical response to the perfect information. If the cost of precautions is sufficiently great, there may be no reduction in insurance coverage (Shavell 1979). In most cases each individual will choose less than complete insurance and take fewer precautions, given the insurance level, than he would under perfect information. Under reasonable assumptions it can be shown that an increase in the effectiveness of the individual's precautions will lower insurance benefits and raise precautions.

CONCLUSIONS

This chapter has presented a basic economic model of the decision to purchase insurance and invest in safety assuming perfect information. The model was extended to show how insurance and safety can be purchased, in effect, by the choice of employers. The assumption of perfect information was then relaxed to allow for moral hazard, and the market response to this type of imperfect information was discussed.

Moral hazard and administrative costs both reduce the amount of insurance that will be purchased, but given these constraints the amount of insurance in principle remains optimal.

If the market can provide the optimal amount of insurance and safety, government intervention, especially mandatory insurance, is not needed and can only make things worse. This conclusion is based on a number of assumptions, however, and whether mandatory insurance is justified when they are removed is the subject of the next chapter. Subsequent chapters will utilize the theory of the market for disability insurance and safety to analyse the design of the benefit payments and other issues affecting both public policy towards, and the operation of, private disability insurance markets.

3
The uneasy case for mandatory disability insurance

INTRODUCTION

In the world represented by the models outlined in Chapter 2, there was no role for government intervention because the market provided the optimal levels of insurance and safety. Despite such economic arguments, disability insurance is increasingly becoming a commodity that individuals are required by government to consume. Workmen's compensation, introduced in Ontario in 1915, was the first example in Canada of mandatory disability insurance for employees. For fifty years there were no others. Then the Canada Pension Plan Disability Benefits were introduced, and more recently there have been suggestions that workmen's compensation be extended to non-work accidents (Saskatchewan 1976; and Manitoba 1977). However, the next expansion of mandatory disability insurance is likely to appear in the form of no-fault automobile insurance. Ontario has no-fault disability benefits (called 'accident benefits') that are compulsory for those purchasing automobile insurance. The Ontario Select Committee on Company Law (Ontario 1978) has recommended an extension of the no-fault concept, and Quebec has already implemented mandatory no-fault insurance coverage. Statutory extensions of liability for product consumers (such as the Saskatchewan Consumer Products Warranties Act) also impose insurance.

In this chapter the economic arguments for mandatory disability insurance are critically examined. Other types of government intervention, such as government administration of insurance, are considered in later chapters.

There are at least five arguments for mandatory insurance:

Redistribution to the disabled. It is argued that the government must force healthy individuals to provide benefits for disabled persons because the latter have a greater need for income.

Misperception. Consumers will underestimate risks and make inappropriate decisions on safety and insurance. Mandatory insurance is required in order to force consumers to purchase the amount of coverage that they would desire if they knew the true risk.

Adverse selection. If insurance is voluntary, high-risk individuals will be most likely to buy insurance. The resulting increase in the cost of insurance may make insurance unattractive for low-risk groups. Mandatory insurance would allow both groups to purchase insurance at average rates, implying, of course, that the low-risk group subsidizes the high risk group.

Externalities. Healthy members of society may feel better off if the disabled are compensated. If the individual chooses not to insure himself privately and becomes disabled, he imposes on others the disutility of contemplating his distress. In this sense everyone can be made better off if mandatory insurance is imposed.

Income-tested government programs. The incentive to insure privately is reduced because of the existence of government welfare programs that provide income for the disabled. It is argued that mandatory insurance is required to offset this disincentive.

The existence of moral hazard, the inability to monitor safety precautions, is not an argument for mandatory insurance. Such a requirement would not eliminate the basic informational problem that leads to moral hazard. Government intervention will not make the insurance market more efficient unless the government can monitor precautions at a lower cost than private insurance carriers, and there is no evidence that governments are more efficient than anyone else in this type of activity.

On closer examination the five justifications for mandatory insurance outlined above turn out not to be very strong.

REDISTRIBUTION TO THE DISABLED

A program that provides benefits for those who are disabled, paid for by those who are healthy, will redistribute income between the two groups. One could argue that there should be more of such redistribution than is implicit in private disability insurance coverage. But how much redistribution is the right amount?

Viewing the system of disability compensation as a system of insurance offers a way out of this dilemma. The argument is similar to Rawls's (1971) theory of justice. Rawls argues that one should analyse theories of distribution from behind a 'veil of ignorance.' That is, the principles by which the society's income is to be divided up should be agreed upon without knowledge of whether one is going to be blessed with significant earning capacity or no earning capacity. The same methodology can be used to analyse policies towards disability. If no one knows whether he is going to be disabled or not, the appropriate policy is to maximize *expected* utility. Such a policy would provide for transfers from those who are lucky to those who are not. This is precisely what insurance accomplishes. It represents an agreement that once it is known who is disabled, each person who is not impaired will transfer income (a premium) to those who are disabled. If this transfer can be done at no cost, the sum of the premiums paid by those who are not disabled equals the benefits received by those who are disabled.

The insurance framework frees one from the difficult question of whether it is better to take from one person and give to another. Rather, one can in effect ask a person the size of the transfer that will maximize his expected utility before he knows whether or not he will be disabled. After an accident the disabled person will prefer more disability benefits to less, but before the accident occurred that person could state an amount that maximized his expected utility, balancing the income that must be given up should he not be disabled in order to provide benefits should he be disabled. If the insurance provided in the market maximizes the expected utility of each person, any attempt to redistribute income to the disabled will lower the expected utility of all members of society. Before knowing that he would be disabled, the disabled person would not support this redistribution.

Compulsory insurance redistributes income between those who are not disabled and those who are, but it redistributes income in other directions too. For example, a mandatory insurance program that charges everyone the same premium, regardless of risk, will obviously favour a high-risk person at the expense of low-risk persons. This type of redistribution may be a consequence of mandatory insurance, but it is usually unintended. Redistribution between those who are not disabled and those who are cannot justify mandatory insurance as long as the objective of the redistribution is to maximize the expected utility of members of society. The rest of this chapter is based on the assumption that that is indeed the objective of public policy towards disability.

MISPERCEPTION

It has been argued that since consumers and workers do not know the risks that they face, compulsory insurance is needed to guarantee the appropriate amount of coverage. So far our analysis has assumed that workers know the probability of their becoming disabled. Supporters of the policies of government intervention described in Chapter 1 (a ban on carcinogenic substances for instance) often argue that the government must act because consumers do not have sufficient knowledge of the risks they face to make a rational decision.[1] And in fact there is growing evidence that the expected utility model is not a particularly good predictor of consumer responses to small probabilities of large loss. One of the predictions of the expected utility theory, for instance, is that a consumer will purchase actuarially fair insurance if he has diminishing marginal utility of income. The gains from insuring against a small probability of a large loss are particularly great if there are no transaction costs associated with acquiring insurance. Nonetheless, people tend not to insure themselves against large losses when probabilities are small.

Economists have long noted the existence of irrational behaviour with respect to risk. Adam Smith discussed behaviour towards risk in his chapter on wage differentials:

the chance of loss is by most men under-valued ... Moderate, however as the premium of insurance commonly is, many people despise the risk too much to care to pay for it. Taking the whole kingdom at an average, nineteen houses in twenty, or rather, perhaps, ninety-nine in a hundred, are not insured from fire ... The contempt of risk and the presumptuous hope of success, are in no period of life more active than at the age at which young people chuse their professions. (Smith [1776] 1937, 107-9)

Because of the lack of home owner interest in subsidized flood insurance, Kunreuther et al. (1978) undertook a comprehensive study of the response of home owners to natural hazards. This was followed by laboratory experiments in which volunteers were asked to make insurance decisions in a number of risky games. The results were surprising:

The analysis of field survey data has revealed the limited knowledge possessed by most home owners residing in hazard-prone areas regarding alternative mitigation measures and relief programs. Furthermore the data demonstrate that a relatively small portion of the home owners have personally protected themselves against potential damage from floods and earthquakes. The laboratory experiments on insurance provide a better understanding of why individuals know and so so little about these hazards. The results suggest that people refuse to attend to or worry about events whose probability is below some threshold. (Kunreuther 1978, 235)

For the most part the failure of the expected utility model in Kunreuther's sample could be explained by the miscalculation of the probabilities, rather than

---

1 Schelling (1978) argues that policies of this nature arise out of 'self-paternalism,' that is, consumers wish to be protected from their own actions.

28 Disability insurance and public policy

the size of the loss.[2] In fact home owners tended to overestimate the *size* of earthquake loss (ibid. 93). In Kunreuther's laboratory experiments the probability and size of losses were both given, yet small probabilities of large losses were not generally insured against. Apparently small probabilities are treated by many individuals as if they were near zero. On the other hand there was some sensitivity to changes in the load factor (the amount by which the cost of insurance exceeds the expected value of benefits) for given probability levels (ibid. 171).

The decisions made by low-income farmers under uncertainty have been subject to considerable analysis because of the implications for agricultural productivity. Risk aversion has been used as an explanation for corp diversification and the slow growth of modern techniques. Roumassett (1976) concludes that low-income farmers behave as if they were risk-neutral. However, this surprising result is also consistent with risk aversion combined with misperception of the risk of low-probability events. These two competing hypotheses cannot be distinguished.

The psychological literature contains some experimental evidence on the evaluation of probability. Tversky and Kahneman (1974) in a study of the incorrect evaluation of uncertain events show how casual estimates of probability can be biased. A very small sample is often taken as representative of the underlying population. In the case of occupational safety this could lead to exaggeration of the underlying risk at small companies that have experienced accidents, just as the risk would be underestimated if no accident occurred. Then again the probability of an event may be estimated from personal experience, so that accidents occurring where few observe them will be underestimated.

In a more recent paper Kahneman and Tversky (1979) present a more thorough analysis of decision-making under uncertainty when probabilities are known. In their alternative to the expected utility model small probabilities are either ignored entirely or weighted too heavily. They point out that their analysis does not explain observed behavior in insurance markets (ibid. 286). Thaler and Rosen (1975), Smith (1976), Needleman (1979), and Viscusi (1978) have found some evidence of compensating differentials for occupational risk, but the differentials may not equal the loss of expected utility evaluated using the true probabilities of accidents.

The misperception argument for mandatory insurance is illustrated in Figure 5. A similar argument could be made for safety regulation if the horizontal axis were relabelled 'safety,' but it would neglect an important consideration. The regulation of insurance does not necessarily alter the person's perception of risk.

---

2 This assumes that we can explain the model's failure in light of the same model. Other models may be more appropriate.

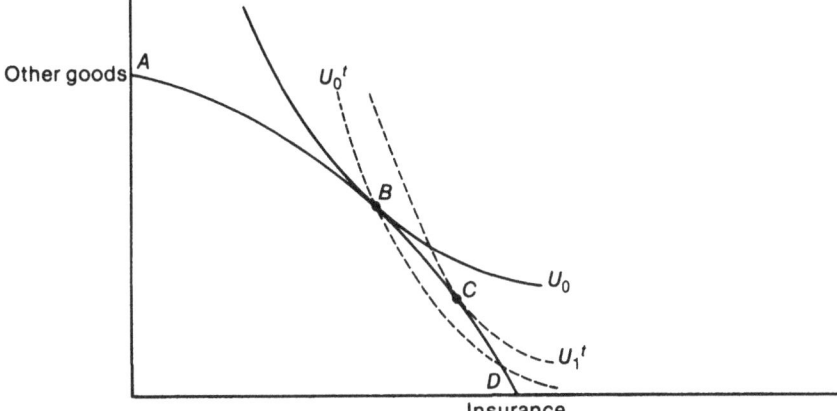

Figure 5: Simple analysis of misperception. A consumer must choose between insurance and other goods within the budget constraint AD. The budget constraint is not a straight line because moral hazard raises the price of insurance as the amount of insurance increases. The consumer believes that he has maximized his utility at point B on indifference curve U_0. However, if he underestimates the risks he faces, his true indifference curve is U_0^t. If he knew the true risk he would choose point C, which is on a higher indifference curve U_1^t. It is sometimes argued that the role of the government is to force the consumer to choose point C by making insurance mandatory.

Consequently he will attempt to adjust other unregulated variables, such as safety precautions, in response to the regulation of insurance coverage. This reaction to government intervention will now be discussed with specific reference to workmen's compensation and occupational safety. Spence (1977) has analysed the effect of misperception on the safety of consumer goods. The model presented here indicates that mandatory insurance or safety may not improve social welfare, in spite of misperceptions.

Market determination of occupational safety and insurance with worker misperception

The effect of misperception and moral hazard will be examined in the context of insurance against occupational risk and safety precautions in industry. The misperception is assumed to be an underestimate of the probability of disability. In other words, the worker maximizes his expected utility but miscalculates the relevant probability. The model is used to determine whether misperception of risk leads to too much or too little insurance and safety or in the absence of government programs. It is then used to determine if government regulation of insurance, such as mandatory workmen's compensation, will increase or decrease the level of safety and the level of utility of workers. (Mathematical note 7).

The model indicates that imperfect information is not necessarily a justification for mandatory disability benefits. If the imperfect information affects the worker's perception of the marginal impact of firm precautions, the imperfect information may produce too much insurance. On the other hand if it only affects the perceived *level* of risk, there will be too little insurance and possibly too much safety. One must know more about the pattern of misperception than we do before government intervention could be justified.

The ambiguity of the effect of misperception on market-determined benefits did not occur in Diamond's (1977) model because he assumed that safety was constant when he analysed the insurance decision and that insurance benefits were constant when he analysed the safety decision. If the level of safety is fixed, an increase in misperception lowers the insurance coverage. If the level of benefits is fixed, an increase in misperception lowers firm precautions. Once both insurance and safety are allowed to vary simultaneously, the results can be ambiguous and sometimes surprising.

Workmen's compensation (benefits fixed)

Workmen's compensation imposes strict liability for occupational disabilities on the employer, with compensation levels set by statute or regulation. Such programs often also include insurance for the employer, but that does not have an important bearing on the misperception issue and is not incorporated in the model. In effect, workmen's compensation is a system of mandatory insurance for workers. In this section the effects of worker misperceptions are considered in light of the fact that the government has intervened to fix benefits, and the response of safety to the level of benefits is analysed. The mathematical derivations appear in Rea (1981).

Oi (1973a, 78) and Diamond (1977, 81) are not necessarily correct in suggesting that workmen's compensation offers a remedy for suboptimal safety caused by excess worker optimism. An increase in disability benefits may or may not increase the firm's precautions. The ambiguity occurs because of two opposing influences on the firm's safety decision. An increase in benefits raises the firm's return to investment in safety by raising the cost of an accident, but it also increases the worker's desire to substitute wages for safety. The latter effect has not been considered in previous studies. It is even possible that an increase in benefits to a level that would provide optimal insurance would reduce the level of safety as a result of the substitution of wages for safety. Rea (1981) demonstrates the circumstances in which an increase in the required level of benefits

Mathematical note 7
The effects of misperception of risk

The effects of misperceptions can be illustrated with a simple model of the labour market. It will be assumed that all firms and employees are homogeneous, an assumption that rules out adverse selection (discussed below) and that employees have no control over the probability of an accident. This latter assumption rules out the problem of moral hazard. It is assumed also that employers provide disability benefits (without administrative costs) if the workers desire them.

Workers are assumed to choose their employers so as to maximize expected utility, which depends on the level of safety, the wage, and the level of disability benefits that are provided. Workers, however, may have incorrect perceptions of the level of risk and the effect of employer precautions on the risk. It turns out that the nature of the misperception is particularly important. A distinction can be made between the perception of the level of risk and the perceived marginal impact of firm precautions. The difference between these types of misperceptions is illustrated in Figures 6 and 7. In Figure 6 the worker perceives that the risks $r(s)$ are lower than the actual risk $a(s)$. The relationship between firm

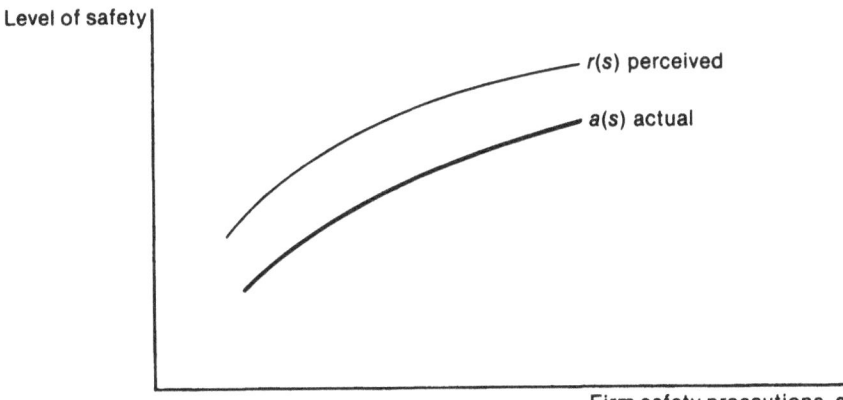

Figure 6: Misperception: $r > a$, $r_s = a_s$

precautions s and safety shifts upwards as a result of the misperception. In Figure 7 the level of safety is initially constant at S_0, but the misperception leads workers to underestimate the impact of firm precautions. Of course both types of misperception could occur simultaneously.

The impact of misperceptions is shown with the model developed above but with the simplifying assumption that worker precautions do not affect safety. Firms are assumed to compete with each other by offering alternative compensation packages, defined by the level of safety s, the wage rate w, and the disability benefit m, so as to maximize the expected utility of workers as perceived by them. The expected utility equals

32 Disability insurance and public policy

$$U^* = r(s)U(w) + (1 - r(s))V(m). \tag{21}$$

The firm must also maximize its profits by varying the number of employees until the marginal revenue product of labour Z equals the cost of an employee:

$$Z = w + (1 - a)m/a + C(s)/a. \tag{22}$$

Notice that the firm is assumed to know the actual level of safety, whereas the employee's perception of it may be incorrect.

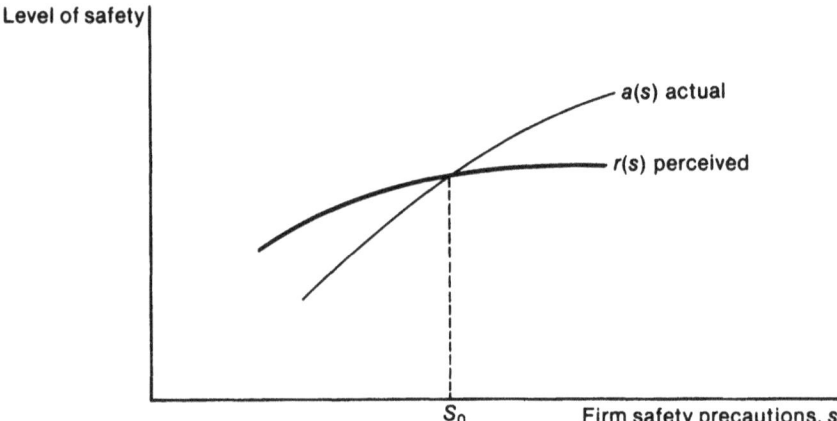

Figure 7: Misperception: $r_s > a_s$

It is shown in Rea (1981) that a market with worker misperception will generate wages, employer precautions, and wages that satisfy

$$U_w/V_m = a(1-r)/(1-a)r, \tag{23}$$

$$ar_s(U-V)/rU_w = C_s - a_s(m+C)/a - a_sZ' \tag{24}$$

Equation 23 suggests that the market level of insurance will be optimal ($U_w = V_m$) only if $r = a$. Equation 24 indicates the safety investment criterion for the firm. Safety is increased until the marginal cost (right-hand side) equals the marginal benefit. The marginal benefit is the lower wage that can be paid if a safer job is offered. The marginal benefit differs from the marginal social benefits because the worker does not correctly evaluate risk.

What is the effect of misperception on the level of insurance and safety provided by the marketplace? If firms cannot control the level of safety, in other words if s is fixed, equation 23 suggests that insurance is suboptimal when workers overestimate the level of safety ($r > a$). However, when safety can be varied the results are not as clear. For example, an increase in worker underestimation of the level of risk with no change in r_s (Figure 6) will reduce insurance coverage but may increase safety. Excess worker optimism leads to a substitution of wages for benefits because implicit insurance rates seem unfavourable. The lower benefits reduce the cost of accidents for the firm, but they may increase the wages workers are willing to give up to pay for firm precautions.

The increase in safety can occur when the misperception alters the perceived level of risk rather than the marginal effect of the firm on risk. In other words, the average perceived return to firm precautions is lowered, but the marginal return remains constant. Therefore, insurance benefits appear to be unreasonably priced, but safety precautions *could* appear to offer an increased return. Since the reduced level of insurance raises the perceived payoff for precautions and more wages are available to purchase safety, safety could increase despite the reduction in the average perceived return to precautions. If worker perceptions are initially correct, a small increase in optimism will definitely lower insurance coverage, increase the wage rate, and reduce safety.

The results described above could be altered if the misperceptions affect the slope of the relationship between s and r, as shown in Figure 7. An exogenous change in perceptions that reduces r_s with r constant decreases safety as expected, but insurance coverage may increase. Insurance coverage will definitely increase in response to a fall in r_s when perceptions are initially correct. Firms reduce safety and increase wage rates as r_s falls. Some of the cost savings resulting from lower safety will be used to purchase insurance because the perceived *level* of risk is initially unchanged. The combined effect of an exogenous increase in r and decrease in r_s must be determined empirically.

---

will *reduce* safety. The reduction in safety occurs because workers are less willing to sacrifice wages for safety when the uncompensated loss $(U - V)$ falls and because workers will accept lower safety in order partially to offset the added insurance premium. The only opposing influence is the increased marginal cost of accidents for the employer because of the higher benefits.

Even without moral hazard, therefore, safety could fall as a result of an increase in compulsory insurance. This possibility has not been appreciated by other researchers. In fact, Diamond's (1977, 81) proof that safety rises when benefits are increased contains an error.[3] The exact nature of the misperception must be known before one can predict the response to mandatory insurance. In particular it must be determined whether the misperceptions affect the perceived level of risk more than the perceived effect of the firm's precautions on the risk.

The crucial role of worker information is shown by considering the situation in which the worker does not alter his estimates of risk in response to the firm's safety precautions. The firm will invest in safety until the marginal cost equals the marginal reduction in accident costs to the firm, without regard to the effect of safety on the wage rate. In this situation there will be no compensating wage differential, and an increase in benefits will raise safety and lower wages. If workers respond to changes in safety, they may prefer to lower safety following an increase in benefits.

---

3 If $V_m > U_w$ (rather than $V_m < U_w$) his equation 25 has an indeterminate sign.

It appears that a reduction in safety following the introduction of workmen's compensation is a distinct possibility. In fact Chelius (1973, 63) finds statistically significant evidence that more generous workmen's compensation levels are associated with higher injury rates, holding other factors constant.[4] This reduction could result from worker substitution of wages for safety or from the impact of moral hazard on worker precautions. Expected utility, evaluated using the actual probability, could fall if the reduction in safety is large enough to overwhelm the positive effect of insurance on utility. If the firm is insured by a workmen's compensation board or an insurance carrier, lack of perfect information on the firm's precautions reduces safety. This additional moral hazard increases the likelihood that expected utility will fall as a result of mandatory insurance.

Many of the distributional effects of mandatory insurance and safety regulations have been ignored in the preceding discussion, in part because of the nature of the assumptions. First, the assumption that workers are homogeneous rules out redistribution between high-risk and low-risk workers as a result of the policies. Second, the assumption of fixed labour supply and the form of the firm's cost function imply that workers will bear all of the costs of insurance and safety regulation. Some of the evidence on the incidence of the payroll tax (Brittain 1972) suggests that this assumption is reasonable.

When economists present models that imply market determination of wages, safety, and insurance, they are often told that many workers have little opportunity to choose between industries and occupations. In fact the model presented here is totally consistent with this view. It focuses on a group of workers who have a perfectly inelastic labour supply in a particular labour market, however narrowly defined. Firms within the industry compete for workers by offering a package that maximizes worker utility for a given cost. The model suggests that all workers, even those with low wages, low disability benefits, and high risk levels, can be made worse off by workmen's compensation. In other words, workmen's compensation does not necessarily lead to a more equitable distribution of income when both premiums and benefits are considered.

Employer-provided insurance for non-employment injuries
An extension of workmen's compensation to cover non-employment injuries seems inevitable simply because insurance coverage is desirable regardless of the source of injury. Manitoba (1977) and Saskatchewan (1976) are considering this extension. In many cases this insurance is provided as part of negotiated fringe benefits, but the amount may be suboptimal because of imperfect information.

---

4 In another study Chelius (1976) found that states with workmen's compensation tended to have fewer deaths from machines than states relying on a negligence standard.

The most obvious distinction between occupational risk and off-the-job risk is that the employer or an insurance company is likely to have no control over the risks associated with non-work activities. Moral hazard is an even greater problem for non-work insurance. In general, the greater the ability of the insured individual to influence the probability of loss, the lower will be the level of insurance and the greater the precautions. Underestimation of risk will also lower the amount of insurance purchased. Therefore, both types of imperfect information, the insurer's inability to monitor non-work precautions and the individual's underestimation of risk, reduce insurance coverage. Given this imperfect information, it would not be surprising to find that coverage for work-related accidents would be more common than coverage for non-work accidents.[5] The only way to eliminate the reduction in care is to legislate the precautions taken by the individual, but the cost of policing all consumption activities would be immense.

Conclusions on misperception
Misperception of risk by consumers and workers has an important effect on the market for insurance and safety. This was shown with reference to worker misperception, but the model is equally applicable to consumer misperception (Spence 1977). The model of the labour market shows that the effect depends on the exact nature of worker misperception. For instance, if employee precautions are fixed, a decrease in the perceived level of risk unambiguously reduces market insurance below the optimal level only if the marginal reaction to employer precautions does not change. Under some assumptions misinformation leads to suboptimal insurance but excessive safety precautions. Mandatory non-work insurance is also likely to reduce precautions taken in leisure activities.

Government policy may not be able to produce both optimal safety and optimal insurance when there is imperfect information. Given the imperfect information, mandatory disability insurance may reduce safety. In plausible circumstances compulsory insurance could even make workers worse off, despite their misperceptions.

ADVERSE SELECTION

An insurance policy priced on the basis of the average individual will be attractive to high-risk individuals and unattractive to low-risk individuals. Only the

---

5 What will be the effect of mandatory insurance coverage for non-work activities? Fair insurance will lower the wage rate by $(1 - a)/a$ per dollar of benefit, net of the premium. A sufficient condition for the insurance to produce a reduction in d is $U_{dw} = V_{dm} = 0$. Utility, evaluated with the actual probability, could fall as a result of the mandatory coverage if d falls sufficiently.

high-risk individuals will buy insurance, so that the sale of the insurance will become unprofitable. This problem, known as adverse selection, is often used as an argument for mandatory insurance, but until the recent work of Wilson (1977) there was no formal analysis of how it would be affected by a compulsory system. Wilson's argument in support of mandatory insurance is reviewed in Appendix A.

Adverse selection occurs when individuals have different probabilities of loss and insurance companies cannot distinguish between high-risk and low-risk individuals. Adverse selection has important implications for the ability of a competitive insurance market to provide optimal insurance. Furthermore, the very existence of equilibrium in these markets is threatened by imperfect information (Rothschild and Stiglitz 1976, and Wilson 1977). Wilson's analysis suggests that mandatory insurance could make both high-risk and low-risk individuals better off in some circumstances but will always make high-risk individuals better off. We do not know if the actual conditions in insurance markets are such that mandatory insurance will make all groups better off.

Economic models of occupational risk generally assume that workers will insure themselves against earnings losses resulting from work-related disabilities. We have seen that imperfect information affects the amount of insurance coverage and occupational safety. Adverse selection further complicates the market for insurance against occupational disability. The inability of the firm or insurance company to distinguish between accident-prone and safer workers affects the allocation of workers among industries, the compensating differential for risk, the amount of disability insurance coverage, and the level of safety.

If workers are *not* able to change the occupational risk by moving between industries, the labour market operates just like an insurance market with adverse selection. The low-risk workers receive incomplete coverage because they have no way of revealing their true risk to employers other than through their choice of compensation packages. In such a case mandatory government insurance could make both groups of workers better off, as shown in Appendix A. The government insurance would most likely be supplemented by private insurance. Therefore, workmen's compensation could be justified by adverse selection within an industry.

However, if workers can choose between industries or occupations with different risk levels, the labour market takes on a dimension not present in an insurance market. A theoretical model to represent the situation has not yet been developed, but the result of such a model would depend to a great extent on the way in which risks vary across individuals and industries. An unanswered question is whether mandatory insurance would improve the allocation of workers between industries and occupations.

EXTERNALITIES

It is argued that the purchase of disability insurance brings returns as well to non-insured members of society, so that mandatory insurance is justified. One of the conditions for optimality of the private market is that individuals consider the effects of their decision on the welfare of others. In the case of insurance and safety, at least two types of externalities could affect the optimality of private decision making. The first type implies that the incidence of disability itself could lower the utility of non-disabled members of society to the extent that they are bothered by the presence of the disabled. The higher the probability of disability, the greater the probability that others will come in contact with a disabled person. If the overall level of safety enters positively into the (non-disabled state) utility function, the safety decision of the individual will not reflect the effect of his decision on other members of society.

A second type of externality occurs when the level of income or insurance received by the disabled person affects the well-being of those who are not disabled. Zeckhauser (1973, 163) observes that expenditures by healthy members of society for those who are ill relieves the healthy person's guilt. If those who are not disabled feel better because the disabled receive insurance, the social return to insurance will exceed the private return, and a mandatory increase in insurance coverage is justified.

Externalities might justify mandatory insurance. The question is, however, whether these really are externalities. Is the apparent altruism really disguised self-interest? The non-disabled person may be willing to transfer income to the disabled in the hope of receiving similar treatment should he too become disabled. Such implicit contracts between members of society provide insurance in the same way that more formal contracts do. If insurance is the motive behind concern for the disabled, there may not be any externalities associated with disability insurance.

INCOME-TESTED GOVERNMENT PROGRAMS

Public programs that provide benefits to those with low incomes have well-known effects on the recipient's supply of labour, but there has been little analysis of how these programs affect the decision to purchase insurance against loss of income, particularly a loss resulting from disability. Does the existence of public income maintenance benefits reduce the incentive to purchase private insurance? This effect of public welfare programs is cited as justification for mandatory insurance coverage (Musgrave 1968, 28; Diamond 1977, 76), whether publicly or privately provided. Similar arguments are used to justify mandatory old-age pensions.

Appendix B examines the effect of public programs on private insurance coverage, identifies the deadweight losses produced by the public programs, and analyses the equity and efficiency implications of alternative tax-back rates in the public programs. On the whole, the existence of public programs does not provide a good argument for mandatory insurance. Welfare programs will discourage purchases of private insurance, but this adverse effect is a price that must be paid for redistribution of income. Mandatory insurance would simply force low-wage earners to pay for their own welfare.

CONCLUSION

Insurance markets are significantly affected by imperfect information, which may lead to suboptimal insurance coverage. However, it does not necessarily follow that government intervention in the form of mandatory insurance will improve social welfare. Moral hazard cannot be avoided by such a policy, nor will misperception be eliminated. The misperception may in practice lead to adjustments in precautions that make individuals worse off. Adverse selection can justify mandatory insurance under certain conditions, but it is not clear whether these conditions apply in reality. Externalities offer another justification for mandatory insurance, but their importance is open to question. Finally, income-tested government disability programs have little effect on the mandatory insurance argument unless one wants to redistribute income away from low-income individuals.

4
Disability benefits

INTRODUCTION

Imperfect information affects not only the level of insurance coverage, as described in the last chapter, but also the structure of benefits. Administrators of a disability benefit program are hampered because they are not able to monitor the exact loss suffered by an individual. They may observe a particular impairment, but not the capability of the disabled individual to earn income. The individual's earning potential depends on his personal characteristics, such as his ability to adapt to the change in his capabilities and the demand for his skills in the labour market. Some impairments, particularly mental disorders and musculoskeletal problems, may be much more difficult to assess. The greater the cost of monitoring a particular individual's lost earning capacity, the more the benefit administrator must rely on the actual loss of earnings as a proxy. As a result, benefits will be designed to increase as earnings fall. This produces another form of moral hazard. The injured person has a reduced incentive to mitigate the loss, so that the size of the loss is affected by the insured's post-accident behaviour.

The extent of moral hazard can be reduced, but only at some cost. Compensation for an injury under common law is based on an expensive process in which all relevant information is gathered, the injured person is subject to close scrutiny, and the award is theoretically tailored to the individual case. The merits of this process will be considered in Chapter 5. At the other end of the spectrum a disability insurance program might only monitor changes in earnings. Usually there is a medical investigation in conjunction with monitoring of earnings, but of necessity the awards are based on general rules and are not individually determined.

40 Disability insurance and public policy

In the previous chapter it was argued that one must understand how a private insurance market operates to decide whether insurance coverage should be mandatory. It was pointed out that the existence of moral hazard does not justify mandatory insurance or a public takeover of the insurance business because the information gaps which lead to moral hazard are present whether or not disability benefits are privately or publicly provided. The effect of moral hazard on the benefit structure will now be considered in general terms. The discussion is applicable to public and private benefits. The effect of benefits on work effort will then be considered in more detail, with emphasis on specific program aspects. Several other issues concerning the benefit structure are also analysed: lump-sum versus periodic benefits, inflation, taxation of benefits, and the integration of separate programs.

This chapter concentrates on income replacement programs, not programs designed to provide or finance consumption of specific goods or services that are required as a result of disability. These extraordinary expenses include medical services, nursing or other types of care, transportation suitable for the disabled, and devices such as wheelchairs. Such items raise the level of insurance that will be required in the event of disability and introduce a number of policy issues not considered in this study. This chapter assumes that medical care is provided by a separate program and that there are no other expenses associated with the disability.

IMPERFECT INFORMATION AND THE SCHEDULE OF BENEFITS

If the extent of disability can easily be determined, the amount of disability benefits provided under an insurance policy will be determined in the manner discussed in the last chapter. Full insurance coverage will be provided by the private market if there is no other imperfect information. In the absence of information on the loss, the benefits will have to be structured on the basis of some other variable which may be controlled by the disabled person. For instance, if earnings loss is monitored rather than loss of earning capacity, there is an incentive for the person to reduce his work if reductions in earnings are partially offset by increased benefits. The resulting reduction in earnings adds to the cost of the insurance and lowers the insurance coverage.

Surprisingly, if the actual loss of earning capacity can be monitored, the ability of the person to influence earnings by altering his effort has no effect on market-provided insurance coverage. Since the optimal benefits will not depend on actual earnings, earnings are not distorted by the benefit structure. Benefits will be lump-sum as far as the income-leisure choice is concerned. This point, made in an insurance context by Spence and Zeckhauser (1971), should be familiar to those who have considered income maintenance programs. Lump-sum redistribution of income is optimal because it does not distort the income-leisure choice. Unfortunately, it is impossible to redistribute income in a lump-sum manner (i.e. without a tax on income) unless some other criterion for redistribution is used besides income.

In practice the extent of loss is imperfectly measured, and the next best indicator, actual earnings, is subject to the insured person's control. Spence and Zeckhauser (1971) indicate how this fact affects the optimal insurance coverage. They conclude that in most cases benefits will increase with the observed variable (earnings loss in our example). The resulting benefit structure depends on the probability distribution of injuries and the response of the disabled person to the incentives created by the benefit schedule. The benefit schedule will represent a compromise between two objectives, full insurance coverage and incentives to mitigate losses.

An analogous problem occurs in the design of income maintenance programs. There are tradeoffs between providing income to a specific group, work incentives, and total transfer costs. The only difference between the insurance problem and the design of an income maintenance program is that the latter requires that one have a social welfare function for comparing utilities of different individuals.[1] The schedule of insurance benefits will be determined in an insurance market when customers maximize their own expected utility.

In the context of medical insurance Zeckhauser (1970) shows that it is theoretically advantageous to have different benefit schedules for different categories of disease, provided it is costless to determine the disease. The appropriate patient share of marginal medical costs would differ between diseases. Disability benefits might be designed to provide a higher earnings replacement ratio for those less likely to be affected by moral hazard. This principle may be evident in the Canadian and United States social insurance systems. The wide range of benefits and tax-back rates between different programs may be appropriate if the costs of determining categories are low and individuals are not able to change categories.[2]

The insurance problem acquires another dimension if resources can be used to acquire information. The advantages of additional information are twofold. First, insurance coverage can be made more complete because the effect of work

---

1 Behind Rawls's (1971) 'veil of ignorance' the determination of the income distribution is essentially an insurance problem because all individuals are identical.
2 For example, welfare programs with high benefit rates and high tax-back rates for mothers with young children may be efficient, provided that they do not include the dissolution of families.

42 Disability insurance and public policy

disincentives on costs is mitigated. Second, whether or not there is moral hazard, the variance in the gap between actual insured loss and benefits can be reduced. Lack of information leads to simple rules for determining benefits. As a consequence benefits rarely equal actual losses. As Williamson et al. (1967) point out, the variance in the relationship between actual and compensated losses is inequitable and reduces a program's risk-spreading effectiveness. The costs of information-gathering procedures include not only direct inputs by administrators, doctors, lawyers, and others but also time and inconvenience for the disabled person. The information-gathering process is discussed at greater length in Chapter 5.

DISABILITY BENEFITS AND WORK INCENTIVES – THE MODEL

There are three general types of disability insurance program. The first type makes no distinction between partial and total disability and requires that an applicant be totally disabled in order to qualify for benefits. The Canada Pension Plan is such a program. One is disabled only if the disability is severe and prolonged, where severe means that the person is incapable regularly of pursuing any substantially gainful occupation. If the disabled person does any work, he will lose all of his benefits (see Chapter 5).

Another type of disability insurance recognizes partial disability but only measures the lost earnings, not the degree of disability. In Ontario the workmen's compensation benefits for temporary disability fall into this category. Benefits are set at 75 per cent of the reduction in earnings.

The third type of benefit is a payment based on a once-and-for-all determination of the degree of disability. The benefit may be paid in a lump sum, such as damages awarded in a suit under common law, or periodically, such as permanent disability benefits under the Ontario workmen's compensation system.

Workers with medical impairments which cause limitations in their capacity to work must consider the desirability of continuing as active participants in the labour force despite their impediments. Functional limitation caused by deteriorating health will affect the hourly wage they can earn and the number of hours they will wish to work, given the additional effort or discomfort imposed by these impairments. Labour market demand determines the wage rates that will be offered to those with physical limitations and the availability of jobs at the prevailing wage rates.

As an alternative to continued employment, workers with health impairments can apply for disability insurance and hope that they will be considered eligible. The desirability of this course of action will depend on the length of the waiting period before benefits can be received, the probability that the application will

Disability benefits 43

be accepted, the amount of benefits that will be received, and the maximum earnings allowed for disability recipients. Unemployment will reduce the costs of an application and may influence the probability that the applicant will be judged disabled.

In order to highlight the role of program criteria on the decision to apply for disability benefits and the labour supply decision, we will first consider the case in which there is certainty that an application for benefits will be accepted as long as no work is done during the waiting period. We also assume that the worker can work as many weeks as he wishes at the prevailing weekly wage rate and that hours per week are held constant.

Disability benefits for total disability

The first type of disability program provides benefits only if the recipient demonstrates no ability to work. The benefit is fixed, usually in relation to the earnings prior to disability. As far as the disabled person's work decision is concerned, the relationship between the benefit rate and the post-disability earnings rate is the relevant comparison. Let K equal the ratio of the weekly benefits to the post-disability weekly wage. This ratio will be higher than the statutory replacement rate if the medical impairment lowers the wage that can be earned.

In any analysis of long-term labour supply decisions there is a problem of graphically representing the constraints and preferences of an individual if the utility of leisure depends on the point in time in which the leisure is available. In order to show the impact of the program parameters a simple one-period model will be used. The one-year analysis exaggerates the influence of the waiting period for those considering an application for permanent disability benefits. In Figure 8 the constraint AEG is applicable in the absence of disability insurance. Utility is maximized at point F. If insurance benefits of m per week are available after a waiting period of D weeks, the labour supply strategy is altered. Anyone choosing to work must do the work at the end of the period in order to avoid demonstrating an ability to work. Anyone wishing more than D weeks of leisure will find it advantageous to apply for benefits, provided that there is no cost of making an application.

The disability program changes the constraint to BEG. Along BE the opportunity cost of an additional week of leisure is the lost weekly wage minus the benefits received, or $(1 - K)w$. This can be called the effective wage w_e. The slope of segment BE is $-1/(1 - K)w$. If the individual does not work at all, the income is $(52 - D)m$, where m is the weekly benefit. The indifference curves are such that the disability program induces a movement from point F to point C, producing a substantial decrease in work. The extent of this work reduction will depend on the parameters of the program, the substitutability of leisure for

44 Disability insurance and public policy

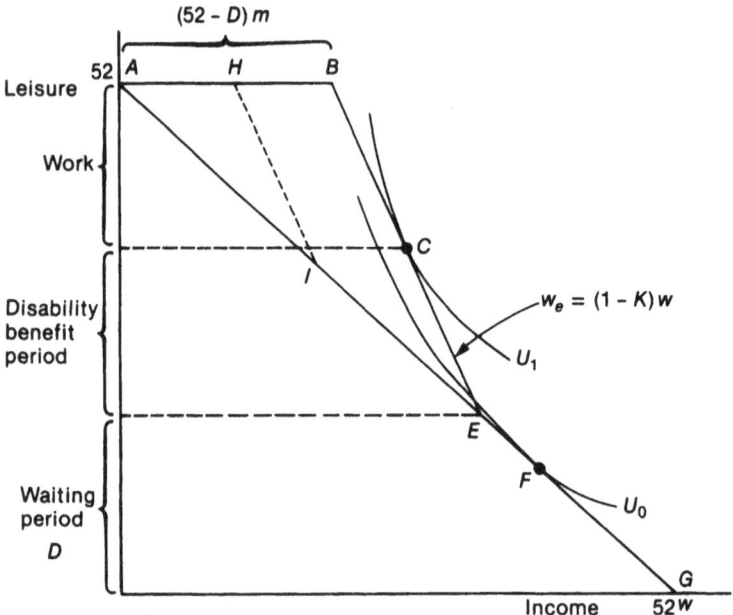

$K = m/w$ = Weekly benefits/Post-disability weekly wage

Figure 8: The labour supply decision: no work allowed while receiving benefits

income, and the relative preference for income. An increase in the benefit rate will raise K and rotate BE around E, making the application for benefits more attractive. If the benefit equals or exceeds the new wage, no work will be done by any benefit recipient. Individuals initially on segment AE will reduce their work as a result of the net effect of the reduction in the returns to work from W to $(1 - K)w$ and an increase in the effective non-wage income from zero to $(52 - D)m$.

The waiting period plays an important role. An increase in the waiting period shifts the constraint inward, such as the movement from BEG to HIG. The effect of this shift depends on the individual. Workers with preferences indicated by the indifference curve in Figure 8 will no longer apply for the program if the waiting period is increased as indicated but will remain at point F. Others will continue on the program but will increase their work if leisure is a normal good. The duration of benefits will fall for these individuals, but the average duration of benefits could rise if those no longer applying had very short benefit duration. Actuarial data (Miller 1978) suggests that the average duration falls as the waiting period increases. An increase in application cost has an effect similar to the response to an increase in the waiting period. The influence of the waiting period (or application costs) will be greatest for those near the normal retirement age, those with temporary disabilities, or those with short time horizons.

In general, an application for disability benefits will be more attractive as the waiting period is reduced, the benefit rate increases, or the market wage falls. The severity of disability will affect not only the wage but also the rate of substitution between income and leisure. That is, the rate of substitution depends among other things on the disutility of working, including any discomfort caused by disability.

The type of program in which work demonstrates lack of a disability will offer no incentive to work for anyone wishing to continue receiving benefits. Work will only be done by those who find it worthwhile to leave the program in spite of a disability. The high implicit tax on work discourages an application for benefits from those with greater taste for income, lower disutility of work, or a higher wage (low K). This group will work more under this type of program than under alternative definitions of disability. However, the number of eligibles who choose not to apply for benefits will be small if K is relatively large.

Disability benefits based on lost earnings

Another type of program compensates workers by making up a fraction, R of the reduction in weekly earnings following the onset of disability. Those who have no earnings receive the maximum weekly benefit m, which is a fraction R of their previous earnings. If the disability reduces the weekly wage because the previous job cannot be performed, $K = R \times$ (Pre-disability wage/Post-disability wage), because $R =$ (Benefit/Pre-disability wage) and $K =$ (Benefit/Post-disability wage), so that K exceeds R when the wage falls. As before, it is assumed that no work will be done during the waiting period in order to avoid prejudicing the application. This implies that the extent of disability is monitored by loss of earnings only for those who have demonstrated disability by not working for D weeks. Since K exceeds R, those wishing to have more leisure than the number of weeks in the waiting period will always apply for benefits.

Figure 9 illustrates the budget constraint for a one year time horizon. In the absence of disability insurance the constraint would be ABC. Following the introduction of the program the budget constraint becomes $FEBC$. If the person worked fewer than $52 - D$ weeks, his effective wage, the marginal return to an additional week of work, is affected by the program. Consider someone who does not work at all (point F in Figure 9). His income equals $(52 - D)m$, the benefits for the remainder of the year following the waiting period. Since work

46 Disability insurance and public policy

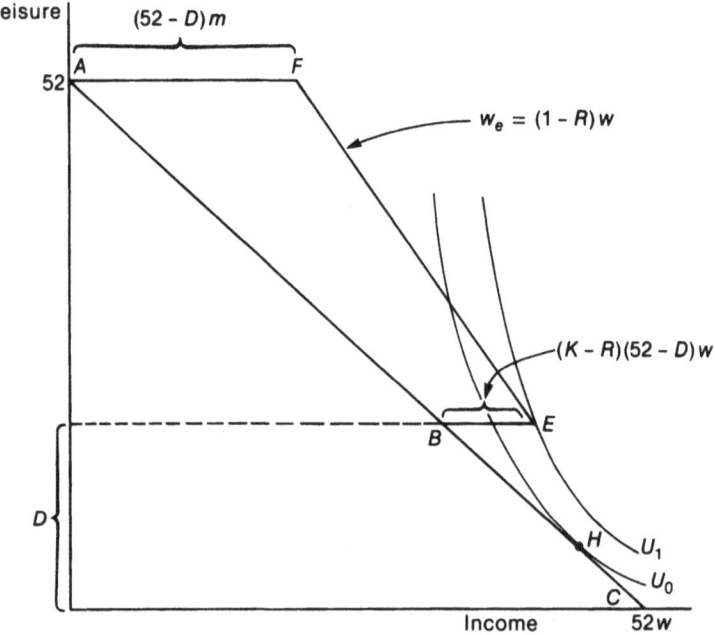

Figure 9: The labour supply decision: benefits fall by fraction R of earnings.

during the period will result in a loss of benefits equal to Rw per week, the effective weekly wage is $(1 - R)w$.

A decrease in the wage rotates ABC clockwise around A and rotates FE around point F. Notice that the gap BE widens as the wage declines, making an application for disability more attractive for a person at a position such as H. An increase in the benefit rate m, coupled with an increase in R, shifts FE out, increasing the slope in absolute value and widening the segment BE. This will reduce work and increase the number of applicants. Rehabilitation increases the wage and produces the opposite effect. It may increase the wage to a point where receipt of benefits is no longer desirable and may also alter preferences by reducing the disutility of work.

Unless total program costs are held constant, it is difficult to compare a program that defines disability based on lost earnings with one that defines disability as complete inability to work. If wages do not fall as a result of disability, K equals R, and the constraints for the two programs are identical. The difference between the two approaches occurs in the timing of work. The

Disability benefits 47

first type of program discourages all work until the end of the decision period, while the second type encourages work in conjunction with receipt of benefits. In practice, however, the results will be quite different, because those who do not work for an extended period are much less likely to retain their skills and their confidence and are less likely to be able to find a job. If wages fall because of the impairment, the second approach will attract more applicants, but it may induce more work because the effective wage $(1 - R)w$ exceeds $(1 - K)w$.

In actual practice an applicant for disability benefits must invest time and resources into his application for benefits, with no certainty that he will receive benefits. If eligibility is determined at the end of the waiting period, he must refrain from working for D weeks before he finds out if benefits will be received. This extra leisure time will be worth less than the forgone income because of the diminishing marginal rate of substitution of income for leisure. The substitution effect therefore determines an important part of the costs of application. Unemployment will eliminate this cost because the waiting period has no opportunity cost for those who are unemployed. Similarly, if unemployment is expected in future periods the desirability of remaining in the labour force is diminished. As a result unemployment will have an important effect on disability applications.

Predetermined benefits

If benefits are determined at the time a disability is established and are not altered by subsequent work, there is little effect on work incentives. If there is a waiting period during which work is avoided in order to demonstrate disability, there is no incentive to work until disability has been determined. Some of the leisure in this period may be substituted for leisure in later periods, but if the required waiting period is long enough, some individuals will be deterred from applying for benefits.

In tort cases the period before the trial is not equivalent to a waiting period for insurance benefits when victory in court is certain because earnings lost during the pre-trial period are eventually restored. There is therefore no incentive to work before the trial. If the outcome of the trial is uncertain, there is a cost of reducing earnings before the trial, and longer delays will discourage lawsuits. This cost to the plaintiff will be small if post-trial leisure is a close substitute for pre-trial leisure.

Once the disability benefit level is established, the recipient's income is raised (but not necessarily above the pre-disability level) by the amount of the benefit, regardless of his actions. There is no distortion of the marginal rate of substitution between income and leisure, but work will fall because of the income effect if leisure is a normal good.

48 Disability insurance and public policy

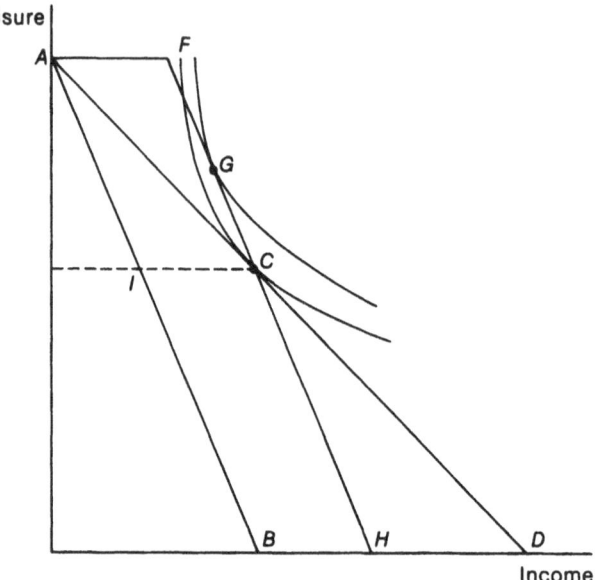

Figure 10: Response to a lump-sum benefit

A partial disability which lowers the weekly wage but does not affect preferences between income and leisure will tend to be overcompensated for by the predetermined-benefit approach. The post-disability work will always be less than the work before the disability if the benefits just offset the decline in earnings, holding the number of weeks worked constant. This is shown in Figure 10 in a one-period context with no waiting period. The pre-disability position is point C, along constraint ACD. An indifference curve is tangent to the line at this point. The disability lowers the wage and rotates the budget constraint to AB. If benefits offset the predicted decline in earnings IC, the constraint becomes FCH. The lower wage will induce substitution of leisure for income (point C to point G). If benefits were sufficiently below the amount IC, the recipient would increase his work as a result of the disability if the income effect were strong enough.

Since the work incentive analysis is substantially the same whether or not the benefits are paid in a lump sum (capitalized) or periodically, court-determined compensation for a disability has substantially the same effect as a periodic program. Figure 10 leads to an interesting prediction about the effect of tort compensation. If the damages are set equal to the lost earnings IC, the plaintiff will always work less after receiving the award. Income will fall despite the court's attempt to maintain income, but the recipient will be better off than before the disability, as shown by the indifference curves. However, this comparison implicitly assumes that there is no uncompensated non-pecuniary loss, no transactions costs borne by the plaintiff, and no change in the relative preferences between income and leisure.

In an analysis of most transfer programs a lump-sum payment such as IC is considered to be efficient because there is no distortion of the marginal rate of substitution between leisure and income. This is not strictly true, however, because the taxes used to finance the transfer may produce inefficiencies. In the context of insurance this program may or may not be efficient, depending on the utility function. The optimal insurance condition requires that the marginal utilities of income in both states of the world be equated, even in the situation in which work is endogenous. If the marginal utility of income is independent of the amount of leisure and the state of the world, the amount IC in Figure 10 would provide too little insurance because the marginal utility of income is higher at G than at C. With this utility function the optimal insurance would leave the person with the same income, including earnings, after the disability. The optimal insurance would exceed the lost earnings at the pervious number of hours worked. In contrast, Figure 10 shows that the tort benefit, which is designed to restore the victim to his previous level of utility, should be less than the reduction in earnings in the absence of non-pecuniary losses.

Tradeoffs between alternative benefit structures
In theory there is an optimal benefit structure for a disability insurance program, but it cannot be determined unless one knows the probability distribution of disabilities, the probability distribution of actual disability for a given observed impairment, and the preference function. The simple insurance model used in earlier chapters is not helpful in choosing a definition of disability because it assumed there is only one type of disability. If this were the case the appropriate benefit structure could easily be chosen.

In the absence of a formal determination of the ideal benefit structure, policy-makers must compromise between a set of objectives for the program. These objectives, which are also those of someone who wishes to purchase disability insurance, are: (1) to provide optimal income replacement for those who have a reduction in earning capacity, (2) to minimize the disincentive to work, (3) to minimize the premiums paid, (4) to offer incentives for rehabilitation, (5) to provide equal treatment for those with equal loss of earning capacity, (6) to minimize the real cost of the insurance, and (7) to encourage optimal precautions against disability. The real cost includes the administrative costs of the program and the deadweight losses caused by the incentives built into the benefit structure.

Some of the objectives are not necessarily conflicting. Features of a program which encourage work and rehabilitation will lower the premium cost, raise the optimal insurance coverage (given the disincentives), and lower the real cost of the program. Horizontal inequities reduce the effective insurance coverage because the extent of compensation for a given loss is uncertain. Other objectives are conflicting. Minimizing the cost of insurance conflicts with providing incentives to take precautions. Since benefits affect precautions, the optimal insurance will be less than complete. Diminishing marginal utility of income makes a marginal reduction in a large loss more valuable than a marginal reduction in a small loss. This suggests that reduction in coverage should take the form of a deductible, in this case a waiting period. Administrative costs reinforce this conclusion, particularly if they are fixed per claim (see Arrow 1963, Shavell 1979).

If the duration of disability is under the control of the individual, an increased waiting period will decrease the disability duration for those who continue to receive benefits. An increased waiting period will reduce insurance coverage but increase work, reduce premiums, reduce real costs, and increase incentives for precautions.

A reduction in the tax on earnings induces additional work for those claiming benefits but will increase the number of beneficiaries. Program costs and real costs may increase (see Rea 1974). As a substitute for use of earnings as a measure of loss of earning capacity, real resources can be invested in information on the extent of an applicant's disability. Work incentives will increase if earnings are not used as a measure of disability, but the information used instead may lead to more errors in assessing disability. If there are errors in the assessment, those with equal impairments may be treated unequally. The greater the uncertainty of benefits for a given loss of earning capacity, the more unattractive an application for benefits becomes. The uncertainty therefore lowers program costs and increases work incentives, but it also leaves uninsured risk. Horizontal equity will most likely be improved if the additional information is used along with measurement of actual earnings.

LUMP-SUM VERSUS PERIODIC BENEFITS

There is growing concern that the lump-sum method of compensation under common law is inappropriate in personal injury cases involving future losses. Instead, it is argued, payments should be made periodically, contingent on the actual amount of the future loss. (Keeton and O'Connell 1965, Ison 1967)

Disability benefits 51

Although these suggestions have been linked to adoption of no-fault compensation, the form of the damage can be separated from the no-fault issue. In fact a form of periodic judgment has been used in nuisance cases,[3] and many countries rely on periodic payments in some or all of their tort cases (Fleming 1969). When the form-of-damage issue is analysed from an insurance perspective, the case for lump-sum awards is much stronger than is generally appreciated.[4] Use of periodic contingent payments in some circumstances could add substantial real costs to the existing cost of accidents.

Despite the long tradition of lump-sum awards in Anglo-American common law, there is increasing pressure for a change to periodic payments. This change is not only accompanying the introduction of no-fault automobile insurance systems, but it has also been recently adopted in at least thirteen states in the United States as an alternative form of payment in medical malpractice actions (Elligett 1979). In the State of Washington the court may order that the award be paid as an annuity not contingent on future events in any civil action.[5] New Zealand led the way with periodic payments for lost earnings as part of a no-fault compensation system (Palmer 1977). Faced with the task of predicting future earnings, taxes, nubility, health, medical costs, and other future conditions, Canadian courts frequently offer a plea for legislation that would provide for periodic payments.[6] Quebec has recently introduced complete no-fault automobile insurance with periodic payments for lost earnings. In Great Britain a Royal Commission (the Pearson commission) recently proposed periodic payments, contingent on the victim's medical condition and the growth of earnings in the economy, for cases involving significant losses of future earnings (Great Britain 1978, 125).

The primary arguments for periodic contingent payment are the uncertain nature of future damages, the resulting future risk that the victim faces with a lump-sum award, and the possibility that the victim might misallocate lump-sum awards. An argument related to the latter issue is that victims will impose costs on other members of society if they misuse their funds and become 'wards of the state.' Generally, periodic payments have been advocated out of concern for

---

3 For example, in *Stollmeyer v. Petroleum Development Co. Ltd.*, [1918] A.C. 498, the defendant was ordered to pay damages 'from time to time' pending elimination of the nuisance. The damage issue arose because the injunction was suspended for two years.
4 Posner (1977, 144-5) mentions the administrative cost and disincentive of periodic payments.
5 Washington, R.C.W. 4.56.240. This provision applies if the plaintiff is totally and permanently disabled.
6 *Andrews v. Grand & Toy (Alta) Ltd.*, [1978] 2 S.C.R.229, at 236; 83 D.L.R. (3d) 452, at 458.

the victim, but as we shall see the victim's interest may not be served by periodic payments.

The uncertainty of damages
Once it is determined that a plaintiff is a victim of a tort, damages must be determined. Unfortunately, this determination usually involves not only quantification of non-monetary losses but also a forecast of future losses. For instance, the court might have to weigh expert testimony and choose an estimate of future wages. In cases in which the probabilities of alternative events are known, it is well established that the expected value of the loss is appropriate. For instance, if the tort results in a 10 per cent probability of a particular disease occurring in the future, the expected loss is one-tenth of the loss associated with the disease (expressed in present value).

A disturbing characteristic of these loss calculations is that after the accident they will almost never turn out to be correct. In all likelihood the loss of wages will exceed or fall below the forecast. If the tort resulted in a 10 per cent probability of a disease, there is a 10 per cent probability that the victim will be undercompensated by 90 per cent and a 90 per cent probability that the victim will be overcompensated. Finally, the original estimate of the probability of the disease might turn out to be incorrect in light of subsequent medical research or future information on the tort victim.

These examples indicate that the recipient of a lump-sum award is faced with a great deal of risk, but not necessarily more risk than he faced before the accident. For instance, his wage income had previously been subject to the fluctuations caused by variations in labour market conditions. Given that the general objective of tort compensation is to return the victim to his pre-existing level of well-being, two criteria must be used to evaluate the method of compensation in risky situations. First, the compensation should minimize the cost of providing a given level of well-being, taking risk into account. In other words, well-being should be maximized for a given cost and one should consider other methods of reducing the risk faced by the victim. One such alternative is that courts make periodic payments contingent on the future condition of the victim. In effect the courts would administer insurance for the victim. Second, the post-judgment risk faced by the victim must be compared with the risks that he would have faced had he not been a victim of an accident. This criterion places a limit on how far tort compensation should go in reducing uncertainty for the victim.

No matter what form damages take, it is not possible to eliminate uncertainty concerning the path that the victim's life would have taken had the accident not occurred. One can only predict that he might have pursued a certain occupation or that he would not catch a certain disease. This remaining uncertainty can be eliminated with insurance. For the totally disabled person, uncertainty over the future earnings in a particular occupation, for example, might be eliminated if it is possible to purchase insurance (an annuity) that provides benefits tied to those earnings. In the disease example described above the victim might purchase a policy which compensates him in the event of disease. The fair premium on such a policy would equal the lump-sum judgment. If the lump-sum payment can be converted into insurance benefits which are contingent on the victim's future condition, the choice between lump-sum and periodic payments reduces to a decision about whether courts or insurance companies are the most efficient administraters of periodic contingent payments. Since there is no reason to believe that courts are particularly well suited to this task, the courts can allow the victim to make the decision between lump-sum compensation and insurance against future contingencies and allow insurance companies to administer the payments.

One must also realize that the defendant might be risk-averse. If the defendant is forced to make contingent payments, he might want to reduce the uncertainty by purchasing insurance. This adds additional costly transactions which could be avoided if a lump-sum payment is made and the plaintiff insures with an institution that is more risk-loving, less likely to become insolvent, and more efficient in administering contingent payments. This argument holds even if the defendant is an insurance company, because not all casualty insurance companies are in the business of selling life annuities and disability insurance.

The argument that victims can eliminate the uncertainty by buying insurance is subject to two criticisms. First, the victim may be irrational and not insure. This argument is discussed in the next section. Second, insurance against contingencies which victims face is not available or is available only at a very high price. The implication is that the public sector can provide this coverage or that the courts can supervise periodic payments by the tortfeasor at a cost that is low enough that the victim prefers periodic payments to lump-sum payments. An analysis of the appropriateness of lump-sum payments thus becomes an analysis of the circumstances under which private insurance markets fail to provide coverage and the extent to which tort victims should be required to be insured against post-accident risks.

Moral hazard
Private insurance markets might not provide insurance coverage because of moral hazard. Moral hazard exists because it is too costly or impossible for an insurer to monitor all the precautions taken by the insured individual or to measure precisely the size of loss, such as the extent of disability. The individual has no

way of demonstrating that he is taking appropriate precautions to reduce the probability of a loss and no way of indicating to the insurer the extent of his actual loss. In fact he has every incentive to behave in a way that exaggerates the reported loss. The extent of moral hazard depends on the responsiveness of individuals to the incentives and the cost of acquiring information on precaution and the size of a loss.

Moral hazard can take many forms. If someone is insured against loss of earnings, he has little incentive to work. If he is insured for medical expenses, he has little incentive to reduce those expenses. If he is insured against failure to remarry, he has no incentive to marry. Fleming (1969, 312) notes that the Germans use the expression 'uncle-marriages' to refer to those who avoid legal marriages in order to maintain survivors' benefits. In contrast to these examples moral hazard is unlikely to exist for life annuities. Some moral hazard is present under the present tort system. Victims have no incentive to mitigate their losses before the trial, as long as their failure cannot be detected. With periodic contingent payments the disincentives may persist for a lifetime.

How can this extreme moral hazard be avoided? First, the victim can sacrifice some of his insurance coverage. The policy by which he insured his future earnings might make up a fraction of the difference between his actual future earnings and the forecast earnings (predicted earnings had the accident not occurred), rather than guaranteeing him the forecast earnings.[7] The policy would be cheaper than one that guaranteed the forecast earnings, in part because of the reduced moral hazard, but would not offer complete insurance coverage and would still affect the insured's incentive to work. A second method of reducing moral hazard is for the insurance company (or representative of the court) to invest in information concerning the insured. It could monitor his health, his efforts at finding a job, and his efforts on the job. The insurance benefits could be contingent on the insured working as long as his health was good. Unfortunately the real costs of the enforcement activity are great, and errors will be made in determining eligibility for benefits. Insurance coverage will be less than complete because the enforcement costs are passed on to the purchaser, inducing him to purchase less than complete insurance, and because errors in determining eligibility make it uncertain whether an earnings loss will be covered by the policy.

Moral hazard usually leads to increased costs of administering insurance, increased costs of supplying a given schedule of benefits, and less than full

---

7 The forecast earnings might be future average earnings in the economy or earnings in a specific occupation.

Disability benefits 55

coverage. Moral hazard may reduce coverage to such an extent that the transactions costs outweigh the advantages of reducing the risk. How is this relevant for the tort victim? Without moral hazard he will be able to use the lump-sum payment to buy insurance. If there is no market coverage for the uncertainties that he faces, moral hazard and transactions costs may explain the lack of a particular type of coverage. However, a court-administered system of periodic contingent payments would face the same moral hazard and the same monitoring costs.

The existence of moral hazard suggests several propositions:

— Given moral hazard, a periodic payment plan that offers full insurance will always cost more than a lump-sum benefit. The lump-sum benefit equals the (discounted) *expected* future loss in the absence of any disincentives, while the periodic contingent payment equals the expected loss plus additional losses induced by the contingent benefits. For instance, if the loss of future earnings resulting from partial disability is predicted to be $10 000 a year and the court orders that benefits equal the actual loss, the resulting reduction in work in response to the 100 per cent tax on earnings will guarantee that the loss exceeds $10 000.

— If there is no market insurance coverage because of moral hazard (and/or the high cost of administering the coverage given the moral hazard), the tort victim with representative risk-aversion will prefer the conventional lump-sum benefit to a periodic contingent benefit of equal cost. In other words, the lack of market coverage demonstrates that the cost of the moral hazard exceeds the advantage of risk reduction for this type of insurance.

— If there is moral hazard in the insurance of the types of risks to which the victim is exposed, the court must determine if the level of risk faced by the victim has changed as a result of the accident. Moral hazard implies that risk reduction can only be achieved at some cost over and above the expected loss in the absence of insurance.

— If the victim faces additional risk as a result of the accident, and the insurance market provides for insurance of these risks, the court need only assess damages equal to the cost of such insurance. If the market insurance is less than full coverage, the victim should be compensated in a lump-sum form for the uninsured risk. In this case periodic payments administered by the court are not necessary.

— If the victim faces additional risk as a result of the accident, but there is no market insurance for this risk because of moral hazard, the court must assess an amount that would compensate the victim for the additional risk. The court should not insure the victim. If the court orders periodic contingent payments in such a case, the cost of these payments will exceed their value to the victim. The victim would always prefer to take the cost of the periodic payments in a lump-sum form.

Adverse selection
The second explanation for a lack of private coverage is adverse selection. A competitive firm that offers insurance against earnings loss with no strings attached will probably attract customers who wish to reduce their work. This poses no problem if the firm can identify those customers whose desire for leisure over income is greater and can charge appropriately higher rates. If not, either all groups have less than full coverage or low-risk groups are forced to choose very low coverage in order to avoid subsidizing high-risk individuals (Wilson 1977).

If adverse selection is a problem in the insurance market, the court could not improve the position of the low-risk person by offering a choice between a lump-sum and a periodic award. Since only high-risk victims would choose the periodic payment, the benefits would be too low to attract the low-risk person. Wilson (1977) shows that in some situations both high- and low-risk persons can be made better off by being forced to purchase partial insurance. If both are forced to purchase full insurance (i.e. accept a contingent periodic award) the low-risk victim may be worse off than with a lump-sum settlement because he is forced to subsidize the high-risk victim. One can conclude that adverse selection may justify contingent periodic payments with no option for the victim, but the gains to the low-risk victim are likely to be small or negative. Since the adverse selection problem is caused by imperfect information on the risk of each individual, it may not be applicable to tort victims, who are subject to close scrutiny when they bring a civil action.

Risks with unknown probabilities
It has been argued that a special problem exists when there is extreme uncertainty concerning the probability of future events. One interpretation of this statement is that insurance companies would have to receive enormous premiums in order to insure some contingencies that cannot be quantified easily. If the insurance company has difficulty quantifying the risks, the court will have the same difficulty.

We concluded above that, given moral hazard and administrative costs, the lump-sum settlement may be preferred by both plaintiff and defendant. If we start with the assumption that the tortfeasor should make good the losses the

Disability benefits 57

victim suffers whatever they may prove to be, can one or both parties be made better off by transferring the risk back to the victim in circumstances in which the probabilities are not known? The victim faces a new risk if the periodic payment is required, the risk that the defendant might default in the future or die without an estate. If the liability is sufficiently great, the defendant has an incentive to rearrange his affairs so as to make the default more likely. For instance, a defendant might be induced to increase his current consumption to avoid the loss of assets in the future. To reduce this type of risk some security must be posted, but how much? In effect the court must determine the amount of liability in advance. The risk-averse defendant who is not planning to default will prefer to pay only this amount in order to eliminate the liability. The victim might prefer to accept this award in lieu of the periodic payments. His decision to accept a lump-sum award will depend upon his perception of the probabilities[8] and the existence of less risk-averse institutions that might insure him on more favourable terms. If moral hazard is taken into account in the court's calculations, as it should be, the greater the moral hazard the more likely the victim would prefer the lump-sum to the periodic payment.

We can conclude that the court cannot escape from the task of making a rough calculation of damages. Furthermore, it seems doubtful that there are many cases in which the security that must be posted would not be sufficient to induce the victim to accept the lump-sum award, or to induce another party to insure the defendant against his liability for future payments. If the plaintiff and defendant agree between themselves to arrange for contingent payments, as was done in some of the thalidomide cases (Morris 1975), the court need not intervene.

Insurance for increased probabilities
Many of the damages caused by a tort are increased probabilities of adverse events. For example, the life expectancy is shortened, the chances of marriage are reduced, and the chances of catching a particular disease, of becoming unemployed, and of contracting future medical costs are increased. It may not be possible to devise insurance that pays off only when an event is *caused* by the tort. 'Premature' death may be a random event, independent of the previous accident. Unemployment may be due to economic conditions, not the reduced skills of the victim. Medical expenses may be incurred for reasons other than the original accident. In some cases it may be possible to attribute a future loss to

---

8 The individual's rate of time preference is irrelevant because he can always buy a fixed term annuity with a lump-sum award.

the accident, but generally it will be extremely expensive or impossible to determine causation. Similar problems occur under workmen's compensation when working conditions increase the probability of cancer in the future.

A possible solution to this dilemma is for the contingent periodic payment to pay off only a fraction of the loss, where the fraction equals the increased probability as a result of the tort divided by the predicted probability. For instance, if the probability of a disease increases from 10 per cent to 15 per cent as a result of the tort, an award payable if the desease occurred would equal one-third of the cost of the disease. This proposal does not provide complete insurance for the victim and is subject to the same criticism that is directed at lump-sum awards, namely that the award will never be exact. Those who acquire the disease because of the tort will be undercompensated and the rest will be overcompensated. It seems preferable to make a lump-sum award based on the increased probability of a loss and let the victim voluntarily buy insurance against the future contingencies regardless of causation. Of course, he will have to use other finds to be completely insured.

Misallocation of lump-sum awards
One of the arguments for periodic payments is that the court must allocate the sum for the victim because he will not rationally utilize the lump-sum award. This argument implies three dimensions to the misallocation: (1) the victim will misallocate his consumption between alternative states of the world; (2) the victim will not make wise investment choices; and (3) he will misallocate his funds between present and future consumption. The first dimension suggests that the victim will not perceive the risk that he faces and therefore will not voluntarily purchase fair insurance. In other contexts such as occupational health this argument may be reasonable, but in light of the uncertainty the victim faces, he should have a better appreciation for life's uncertainties than the average person.

The second dimension suggests that the victim who is not used to managing an investment portfolio will not know which assets to acquire. Many writers have pointed out that there are professional managers of other people's money who can provide this advice. In any event, the theory of efficient capital markets suggests that no special talents are required to be an investor. In the absence of inside information a dartboard may be a reasonable tool for making investment decisions.

The third dimension to the misallocation argument implies that the victim will not make an appropriate decision concerning saving. His time horizon might be so short that he immediately consumes all the award. It is not surprising that many recipients of lump-sum awards consume at a more rapid rate than the court predicts because not all victims will initially have as low a rate of time

Disability benefits 59

preference as the market rate of interest. No rigorous studies have been done on the use of lump-sum awards,[9] but it has been stated that 'it is an open secret among plaintiff's lawyers that the awards they recover for their clients are rarely invested and used so as to provide for the injured person's long-term needs' (Keeton and O'Connell 1965, 354). Some observers have argued that the court should prevent this behaviour by offering the award in a periodic form, such as a life annuity. The misallocation of funds may not be prevented by this device if the law permits the victim to borrow against future income. Furthermore, this device does not address the issue of uncertain future events other than life expectancy.

The misallocation argument acknowledges that, given a choice between lump-sum or periodic payment, victims will usually choose lump-sum payments. This has been the experience in countries such as Germany where both types of judgment are permitted (Fleming 1969, 297). In the United States periodic settlements are rare. This is not surprising. If the conversion of lump-sum award to a periodic award takes into account the administrative costs of the award and the added cost imposed by moral hazard, the victim is rational to choose the lump-sum award. He can always insure voluntarily against contingencies that are insurable at favourable rates.

The court might be interested in the manner in which the victim allocates his award because paternalistically it wishes to make decisions for the victim or because it fears that the victim will become eligible for welfare benefits if the award is 'misused.' This point seems to suggest that society has a right to allocate the funds for the victim, but this argument falls apart when one realizes that other members of society are allowed to make irrational decisions and decisions that could make them eligible for welfare. They can also make 'foolish' decisions concerning consumption and investment in human or non-human capital. Compensation for the tort victims should include providing the same freedom of choice that he previously enjoyed.[10]

Other considerations

Distributional consequences
Startling as it may seem, a great deal of the concern over lump-sum payments is that there might be 'windfall gains' to survivors if the victim does not live as

---

9 Harper and James (1956, 1304) cite a study of the U.S. Railroad Retirement Board which claimed to show that lump-sum payments were not used as a 'stable substitute for the loss of wages.' There is a similar finding in Morgan et al. (1959).
10 Trust funds or other arrangements can always be made in the case of minors and others who are clearly not capable of managing their own affairs.

long as expected (Elligett 1979, 131). Funds awarded for medical care would not be needed in this event. The possibility that the victim will suffer a windfall loss because he lives longer than expected is largely ignored. The windfall argument is equivalent to claiming that consumers who buy fire insurance and do not have a fire suffer a windfall loss of the premium. Nevertheless, this kind of thinking seems to have been the basis for some laws in the United States allowing periodic judgments.[11]

Administrative efficiency
The process under which fault is determined and damages are awarded is extremely costly, but it would be even more costly if continual review of the cases would be required. Some of these monitoring costs are the result of moral hazard, described above.[12]

Other costs
Accidents often cause damages of a very personal nature. Before trial the victim is usually investigated and often put under surveillance in order to document intimate details about his personal life. During the trial these details are publicly discussed. This process imposes real costs on the victim, who suffers embarrassment and loss of privacy. Periodic payments would prolong this process for as long as the damages persist. The difficulties inherent in this process can be seen by studying welfare administrators' experiences with provisions such as the rule that disqualifies a women from receiving welfare if there is a man in the house. If the principle of restoration to the original position has any meaning, the victim would have to be compensated for these additional costs.

Integration with tax and transfer programs
The victim of a tort may be eligible for other forms of compensation such as disability benefits under the Canada Pension Plan, private disability insurance

---

11 Cal. Civ. Proc. Code, § 667.7(f), states that it is the intent of the legislature to eliminate 'the potential windfall from a lump-sum recovery which was intended to provide for the care of an injured plaintiff over an extended period who then dies shortly after the judgment is paid, leaving the balance of the judgment award to persons and purposes for which it was not intended.'
12 Morgan (1959, 20) found that lump-sum workmen's compensation benefits tended to be chosen over periodic benefits in those cases in which the extent of disability was more doubtful, such as back injuries. In these cases the insurance companies pressured for lump-sum settlements, presumably to reduce monitoring costs, and the victims settled to avoid the high cost of continually demonstrating that they were disabled (Morgan et al. 1959, 55).

Disability benefits 61

benefits, and income-tested welfare programs. If the tort award offers full compensation, the victim will be overcompensated. This is not simply a distributional problem. Those who are overcompensated in the event of an accident caused by someone else's negligence are, in effect, overinsured. They could be made better off by redistributing their income between their healthy and disabled states of the world.

Although it is often argued that periodic payments are required in order to integrate tort benefits with other benefits, the integration of insurance benefits and tort awards can be accomplished without moving towards periodic awards. If public or private disability insurance only covers accidents that do not lead to a civil action, or if collateral benefits are deducted from the award, there is a reduced incentive to bring a civil action. Therefore, the insurors should be given the right to bring a civil action against the tortfeasor (a subrogation right). This could apply to public insurance (CPP) or welfare as well as private insurance. For instance, the Ontario medical insurance system (OHIP) has subrogation rights in tort cases.

Taxes pose a more difficult problem because the taxes paid over the lifetime of a recipient of a lump-sum award will differ from the taxes that he would have paid on his earnings. The award is tax-free, but the investment income from the fund is taxable. If taxes are ignored in the calculation, the victim may be better or worse off than before the accident, depending, as we shall see, on a number of factors. It is possible for the tax implications of the award to be taken into account in order to guarantee that the victim is restored to his previous after-tax position, but the government would have to be a party to the suit in order to equate the total award to the total social cost of the accident.[13] It is no doubt simpler to make periodic payments to the victim which would be automatically taxed on the same basis as other income.[14]

Income-tested welfare programs such as disability insurance pose other problems. If there is no asset test, the welfare benefits will be reduced because of the income earned on the principal[15], but there may be overcompensation in a lifetime context. If there is an asset test, such as under GAINS-D in Ontario, there

---

13 If the taxes for the victim were higher because of the lump sum, the government would have to pay the victim the difference. If the taxes were less, the defendant would pay the government.
14 Medical expenses would be deductible, and so on. The Pearson Commission claims that one of the advantages of periodic payments is to avoid the investment income surtax (Great Britain 1978, 124).
15 Since the income-tested programs tax nominal income, including an amount that is offsetting inflation, the real principal is in fact taxed.

is an incentive for the victim to increase his consumption in the early years, and again there will be overcompensation as well as misallocation of his consumption stream. This incentive exists for all members of society and is an example of the moral hazard associated with insurance against low income. However, it is not an important reason for eliminating the lump-sum tort settlement.

Voluntary and mandatory periodic payments
Although many advocates of periodic payments advocate that they be mandatory, there is always the possibility that both forms of payment might coexist on a voluntary basis. However, the three parties involved, the plaintiff, the defendant, and the court may disagree as to the form of the payment. If courts are required to give periodic awards, the plaintiff with a preference for a lump-sum award will have less bargaining power in his negotiations with the defendant over a settlement. The plaintiff cannot convert the periodic award back into a lump sum if the benefits are not assignable. The plaintiff in this case will be willing to sacrifice some of the award in order to gain a lump-sum settlement. Those who advocate mandatory periodic payments because they believe that lump-sum awards are misallocated will make plaintiffs worse off as long as settlements can still take a lump-sum form.

Conclusions
Most of those advocating periodic payments, particularly in the no-fault context, do so out of concern for accident victims and a belief that the award will not coincide with the actual loss. On closer inspection, however, it seems that on average the victim will never be made better off (for a given cost) if the court makes awards periodic and contingent on future losses. On the other hand the availability of private insurance guarantees that lump-sum awards can always be converted to periodic or contingent payments if risk reduction is desired.

The other argument for periodic payments rests on paternalism. Advocates of periodic benefits feel that the victim will be made better off by receiving periodic benefits, even if he prefers a lump-sum award. The general conflict between paternalism and free choice cannot be settled here, but the paternalistic approach suffers from two crucial inconsistencies when applied to the form-of-damages issue. First, the victim is not made whole if his stream of lost earnings, against which he can borrow some amount if he wishes to increase his present consumption, is replaced with a stream of payments against which he cannot borrow. Second, as long as there is the possibility of a lump-sum settlement and the victim prefers lump-sum benefits, the threat of court-imposed periodic payments will lower the lump-sum settlement, clearly making the victim worse off.

The current system in which tort awards are made several years after an accident is a system of partial contingent payments. The award consists of payment for actual losses up to the date of the award and payment for expected losses in the future. The delay in the court proceedings is often justified on the ground that more information is needed on the extent of loss. The delay serves to insure the victim against the losses that are observed before the trial. In most cases all the losses occur before the trial. Moral hazard is created because the plaintiff has an incentive to exaggerate this loss. Reducing the delay to trial increases the risk that actual losses will not be covered but reduces the moral hazard. The optimal length of delay between accident and trial may be shorter than current practice.

INFLATION

Inflation poses problems for any compensation system, whether it be lump-sum or periodic. The recipient of a constant periodic payment will suffer declining real income as rising prices reduce the purchasing power of his benefit. The problem is particularly severe for those receiving benefits over long periods. In Table 1 a recipient of $10 000 a year facing a 7 per cent annual inflation will be able to purchase only $2765 worth of goods (in Year 1 prices) in the twentieth year.

In tort law the principle of *restitutio in integrum* requires that damages be calculated so as to return the victim to the position he enjoyed before the accident. In the absence of taxes this implies that the award must provide an amount in each future year which equals the lost earnings. Since the prediction of future earnings is based on current price levels, it is reasonable to assume that the future earnings will increase in each year along with the cost of living. The Supreme Court of Canada recently acknowledged that inflation must be built into the damage calculation,[16] but it did not understand that the forecast rate of inflation must be consistent with the rate of interest used to discount future losses. After the relationship between the interest rate and inflation is explained, it will be shown that courts need not explicitly forecast the rate of inflation unless the effect of inflation on taxes is to be considered.

Interest rates can be thought of as a mechanism for enticing consumers to forgo consumption today in exchange for consumption in the future. Consider the simple case of someone who is loaning $100 for one year at 3 per cent interest. In the absence of inflation the 3 per cent interest is the reward for

---

16 *Andrews v. Grand & Toy (Alta) Ltd.*, [1978] 2 S.C.R. 229, at 258.

TABLE 1

Annual consumption for recipient of $10 000 a year for twenty years, 7 per cent inflation, 10 per cent interest rate

Year	Disability income	Disability income year 1 prices	Constant purchasing power consumption	Saving	Interest 10%	End of year assets
1	10 000	10 000	6 013	3 987	0	3 987
2		9 346	6 434	3 566	399	7 952
3		8 734	6 884	3 116	795	11 863
4		8 163	7 366	2 634	1186	15 683
5		7 629	7 882	2 118	1568	19 369
6		7 130	8 434	1 566	1937	22 872
7		6 663	9 024	976	2287	26 135
8		6 227	9 656	344	2614	29 093
9		5 820	10 332	−332	2909	31 670
10		5 439	11 055	−1 055	3167	33 782
11		5 083	11 829	−1 829	3378	35 331
12		4 751	12 657	−2 657	3533	36 207
13		4 440	13 543	−3 543	3621	36 285
14		4 150	14 491	−4 491	3629	35 423
15		3 878	15 505	−5 505	3542	33 460
16		3 624	16 591	−6 591	3346	30 215
17		3 387	17 752	−7 752	3022	25 485
18		3 166	18 995	−8 995	2549	19 039
19		2 959	20 325	−10 325	1904	10 618
20		2 765	21 748	−11 748	1062	−68

NOTE: The calculations assume that the interest is paid on the assets held at the end of the previous year and prices rise at the beginning of each year. Disability income is received at the beginning of each year.

delaying consumption for one year. If prices rise 7 per cent by next year, the $100 loan plus $3 in interest will be worth 7 per cent less in terms of this year's purchasing power. The consumer is put in a position of giving up $100 in consumption goods to have the equivalent of $103/1.07 = $96.26 in consumption goods next year. He may be induced to consume this year rather than lending on these terms. The borrower of funds on these terms may be induced to borrow more because he can repay the loan with dollars that are worth 7 per cent less. Since lenders are less willing to lend and borrowers are more willing to borrow, the interest rate must rise above 3 per cent to equate the supply and demand for loans. If the consumer was willing to lend at 3 per cent interest in the absence of inflation, he will be willing to lend at (roughly) a 10 per cent rate of interest if inflation equals 7 per cent. At the end of the year the $100 plus

Disability benefits 65

$10 interest has a purchasing power equal to $110/1.07 = $102.08 in today's prices, roughly 3 per cent more than at the beginning of the year. The borrower is willing to pay 10 per cent because he can repay the loan with dollars that are 7 per cent less than when the loan was made. Economists differentiate between the *nominal* interest rate and the *real* interest rate, the latter being corrected for inflation. In this example the nominal interest rate is 10 per cent and the real interest rate is 3 per cent.

A similar process is at work in the economy as owners of wealth decide on what assets to hold. Alternative assets offer varying degrees of protection against inflation. For example, if one owns property which provides a rent that is revised frequently, the annual rent will increase more or less in line with the cost of living. In other words, the *real* return on the investment is relatively constant. On the other hand if one buys a bond, the interest earned will be fixed in *nominal* terms. As prices rise fewer goods and services can be purchased with the fixed interest on a bond. Furthermore, when the bond is retired, the purchasing power provided by the principal will be lower because of inflation. Rational investors will choose between the alternative types of assets based on the real rate of return expected. In order to know the real rate of return from assets such as bonds, they must forecast the rate of inflation. The higher the expected rate of inflation, the higher must be the nominal interest rate on the bond in order to entice investors to hold bonds. The market-determined interest rate on bonds will be roughly the sum of a long-term real rate of return and the expected rate of inflation. Since the expected rate of inflation cannot be measured directly, a reasonable estimate of the expected real rate of return is the amount by which interest rates have exceeded inflation in the past. For example, the rate of return on long-term Government of Canada bonds averaged 2.2 percentage points above the rate of inflation between 1955 and 1977.

Once one understands the relationship between interest rates and inflation it is easy to see that the estimate of future inflation is not needed by the court. Consider an individual whose loss one year from now is estimated to equal $10 000 in today's prices. If inflation is forecast to be 7 per cent, the plaintiff will need $10 700 next year to be restored to his former position. If the market interest rate is 10 per cent, the present value of $10 700 is 10 700/1.1 = $9727. If instead we simply calculate the present value of $10 000 using a real rate of return of 3 per cent, we get substantially the same result without considering the rate of inflation: $10 000/1.03 = $9709. The slight difference between these two figures is eliminated if the interest is continuously compounded. Alternatively, we can achieve an exact result if we recognize that the interest payment (as well as the principal) will have lower purchasing power after a year of inflation. If r is the real rate of return and p is the rate of inflation, the interest rate must equal $r + p + (r \cdot p/100)$ to guarantee a real rate of return equal to r. For example, if the rate of inflation is expected to be 7 per cent and the real rate of return is 3 per cent, the interest rate must equal $7 + 3 + (7 \times 3/100) = 10.21$ per cent.

Table 2 shows that the amount of consumption that can be maintained with an initial capital fund of $148 775 is the same regardless of inflation because of the response of interest rates to inflation. In the absence of inflation this fund can sustain $10 000 a year in consumption for twenty years with a 3 per cent rate of interest. Alternatively, the same fund can sustain the same consumption under 7 per cent inflation if the interest rate equals 10.21 per cent. The last three columns in Table 2 represent the pattern of assets, income, and consumption if nominal consumption rises with the price level but real annual consumption remains constant. The example in Table 2 also shows that when inflation is expected (and realized) assets must be accumulated in the earlier years to provide for high-cost future consumption.

We can conclude that exactly the same capital sum will be calculated if either of two methods is used: if $10 000 is capitalized at a real rate of 3 per cent or if $10 000 is increased by 7 per cent a year to account for inflation and the resulting series is discounted at a rate of 10.21 per cent. However, it is crucial that the forecast rate of inflation used to inflate the $10 000 annual sum be the same rate of inflation as is implicit in the interest rate. This is where the Supreme Court judgment made a crucial miscalculation in *Andrews*. Mr Justice Dickson noted that current rates were approximately 10½ per cent and subtracted a forecast rate of inflation of 3½ per cent, producing a 7 per cent real rate of discount. The use of this excessively high real discount rate substantially reduced the awards. For instance, in *Andrews* the pecuniary loss would be $1 109 373 with a 3 per cent discount rate, compared to $641 713 with a 7 per cent discount rate. The 3½ per cent inflation forecast is totally inconsistent with the rate of inflation, which participants in the market were predicting in 1978 when interest rates were above 10 per cent. This type of error will occur in the use of the second method unless the (nominal) discount rate reflects the same forecast of inflation that is used to inflate future losses.

The confusion over expected rates of inflation can be ignored altogether if the courts use a real rate of discount which reflects historical experience, such as 2 to 3 per cent. The damage assessment process could be greatly simplified by a Supreme Court ruling that a particular real rate is reasonable for all cases. It is extremely inefficient for economic evidence to be heard on the historical real rate of return in every case.

The suggestion that inflation be considered implicitly (by using a real rate of discount) rather than explicitly is only correct if taxes are not considered. In the

TABLE 2

Consumption supported by lump-sum payment

	No inflation			7% inflation		
Year	End of year assets	Interest 3%	Consumption	End of year assets	Interest 10.21%	Consumption constant purchasing power ($10 000 year 0 prices)
0	148 775			148 775		
1	143 238	4463	10 000	153 265	15 190	10 700
2	137 535	4297		157 464	15 648	11 449
3	131 661	3950		161 291	16 077	12 250
4	125 611	3768		164 651	16 468	13 108
5	119 379	3581		167 436	16 811	14 026
6	112 961	3389		169 523	17 095	15 008
7	106 350	3191		170 773	17 308	16 058
8	99 540	2986		171 027	17 436	17 182
9	92 526	2776		170 104	17 462	18 385
10	85 302	2559		167 800	17 368	19 672
11	77 861	2336		163 883	17 132	21 049
12	70 197	2106		158 093	16 732	22 522
13	62 303	1869		150 135	16 141	24 099
14	54 172	1625		139 678	15 329	25 786
15	45 797	1374		126 347	14 261	27 592
16	37 171	1115		109 725	12 900	29 522
17	28 286	849		89 340	11 203	31 588
18	19 135	574		64 662	9 122	33 800
19	9 709	291		35 098	6 602	36 166
20	0	0		-15	3 584	38 697

NOTE: The calculations assume that the interest is paid on the assets held at the end of the previous year and prices rise at the beginning of each year. End of year assets equal the previous year's assets plus interest minus consumption.

next section it is shown that the impact of taxation depends on the rate of inflation. Therefore, a forecast of the rate of inflation may have to be made, but it is crucial that it be consistent with the inflation forecast implied by the level of the market interest rate.

If future rates of inflation equal the expected rates of inflation, the predicted real rate of return will be realized. The victim with a capital fund can divide his consumption equally over his lifetime, as shown in Table 2. The recipient of a constant periodic payment, such as workmen's compensation benefits, can accomplish the same result by saving a portion of his income during the first part

68 Disability insurance and public policy

of the period and dissaving thereafter. In Table 1 it is shown that a $10 000 annual payment can support $6013 in consumption a year measured in Year 1 prices if interest rates rise from 3 to 10 per cent as inflation rises from zero to 7 per cent. Given the assumptions in the table (7 per cent inflation and 10 per cent interest rate) this is accomplished by saving during the first eight years. Higher rates of inflation and interest rates would require that the recipient save for a longer period, but the consumption would remain the same as long as the real rate of return (2.8 per cent, or roughly 10 per cent minus 7 per cent) remains the same.

Table 1 shows that the real value of $10 000 for twenty years is reduced by 40 per cent because of the inflation. Alternatively, the numbers indicate that the constant annual payment would have to be increased by 66 per cent[17] in order to provide the Year 1 consumption equivalent of $10 000 per year. Unfortunately, even if the benefits were correspondingly increased, the constant consumption plan could be foiled by unanticipated changes in the rate of inflation. The term 'unanticipated' refers to an increase in the rate of inflation which is not built into the market-determined interest rate. For instance, if the person in Table 2 purchased a twenty-year annuity when the interest rate was 3 per cent and expected inflation was zero, he would suffer a 40 per cent reduction in his standard of living if inflation rose to 7 per cent. The recipient of this constant annuity and the person supported by a lump-sum benefit are more vulnerable to such changes than recipients of other types of income. For example, wages have increased in the past more or less in line with the cost of living.

It seems obvious that the recipient of a disability pension should have insurance against unanticipated inflation. In other words, the benefits should be 'indexed.' The need for indexed benefits cannot generally be met by private insurance companies because they cannot hold indexed assets that will offset the indexed liabilities (see Pesando and Rea 1977). Government programs face no such constraint because the government will not go bankrupt as a result of short-run unanticipated inflation. For instance, there is no reason for the lack of indexing of Ontario's workmen's compensation benefits; such benefits are indexed in Quebec and British Columbia.

Concern over inflation probably motivated some of the suggestions that tort compensation be made periodic. The court could eliminate the inflation risk for the plaintiff by ordering that the defendant pay the actual future losses. This would expose the defendant to the inflation risk, a risk that insurance companies are not at present willing to bear. Since the value of the defendant's assets will not necessarily fluctuate with changes in prices, the victim may not receive any

---

17 This equals ((10 000 ÷ 6073) − 1) 100.

Disability benefits 69

compensation if unanticipated inflation is great enough. A possible solution is for the government to establish a fund that receives the lump-sum awards, calculated as above, and converts them into annuity payments which are adjusted for the cost of living. The payments should not be contingent on other events, for reasons explained above. The government fund would face periods of negative net liability but would not go bankrupt like a private insurer in similar circumstances. Over long periods the government fund would break even as long as the forecast real rate of return is realized.

The draft of the U.S. Uniform Periodic Payments Act (UPPA) proposes an interesting partial solution to the indexation dilemma. The draft bill specifies that the annual annuity should be raised by the difference between the one year U.S. Treasury Bill rate and 3 per cent. This procedure, if modified slightly, would in effect adjust benefits in each year according to the expected increase in cost of living, assuming that 3 per cent is the expected real rate of return.

The modification of the UPPA approach would revise the annual benefit upwards such that

$$Y_j = Y_{j-1} [1 + (i_j - r)/(1 + r)],$$

where Y_j is the nominal benefit in year j, i_j is the nominal rate of interest on one year bonds in year j, expressed as a decimal, and r is the expected real rate of return, expressed as a decimal.

Rea (1979) shows that such an annuity would duplicate what a consumer would consume in each year if he desired to consume the same real amount in each year of his life. For this reason the annuity is called a Consumption Stabilizing Annuity (CSA). The procedure implicitly revises the consumption plan upwards whenever there is unanticipated inflation. Real consumption will turn out not to be equalized, even if on average there is no unanticipated inflation over the victim's lifetime.[18] The risk of unanticipated inflation still falls completely on the victim. The seller of such an annuity bears no risk, as long as he purchases one year bonds with the proceeds of the annuity.

---

18 After each year in which unanticipated inflation occurs, the real consumption is reduced in the current year and in all subsequent years. If inflation is less than anticipated in the future by an offsetting amount, real consumption will rise again, but lifetime real consumption is still lower than intended. The losses do not cancel out because a portion of the capital loss that occurred as a result of the unanticipated inflation was previously realized and used for previous consumption. If unanticipated inflation equalled 1 per cent in one year and was offset by 1 per cent unanticipated deflation in the next year, lifetime real consumption would be reduced by 1 per cent of one year's consumption.

The Consumption Stabilizing Annuity diverges from a traditional annuity fixed in nominal terms in three ways. First, it is tied to short-term interest rates rather than the long-term rate at the date of purchase. This lowers the risk (and possibly the real return). Second, the annuitant does not have to calculate the amount of real consumption that can be sustained over his lifetime. At each moment the annuity provides exactly the amount of real consumption that can be sustained, given the expected real rate of return. The annuitant can simply consume all the annual annuity benefits, relying on the intermediary to make all the calculations. Third, the annuitant does not have to re-invest or borrow small amounts each year. The reduction in these transactions costs for the annuitant may be substantial. These advantages can be achieved without any risk to the seller of the annuity. Therefore, the CSA could be offered by disability insurors and private pension funds.

Policy-makers should carefully consider some public support for private indexed annuities (as opposed to the CSA). The decision to offer indexed annuities should be made in light of the uncertainty faced by all citizens, not just tort victims or disabled pensioners. The uncertainty of the future real purchasing power of a disability pension (or any other pension) greatly reduces the risk-reducing effectiveness of the insurance. Wage-earners face much less inflation risk than those receiving fixed annuities. The apparent inability of private insurance companies to offer indexed benefits is a strong argument for some government action, but this does not necessarily imply that the government should run all insurance and pension programs. It would be sufficient for the government to provide indexed annuities to insurance companies or to re-insure the companies as suggested by Pesando (1979). The relative ease with which this could be accomplished suggests that a decision to move toward government-administered disability insurance would have to be justified on other grounds.

TAXATION OF DISABILITY

The tax treatment of disability benefits and premiums for disability insurance is important because taxes can encourage or discourage purchases of disability insurance and significantly alter the percentage of net income that is replaced by an insurance policy. In Canada, the tax treatment of government benefits, private benefits, and awards in negligence cases is inconsistent. The Canadian tax treatment will now be reviewed after some general principles are discussed.

An insurance policy requires that a premium be paid in return for benefits in the event of disability. If premiums are not tax-deductible and benefits are subject to taxation, the same income is taxed twice. Insurance against contingencies would be discouraged relative to precautionary saving under this approach.

Disability benefits 71

It makes sense either to allow premiums to be tax-deductible and tax the disability benefits or to allow benefits to be paid tax-free provided premiums are not deductible. The tax revenue under the first approach would be smaller because the taxable income of those who are disabled is likely to be lower than the income of contributors and because the insurance company's load factor (margin for cost and profit) is not taxed.

The Carter Commission advocated the first approach (Canada 1966, 438) for workmen's compensation and sickness and accident insurance. There are several reasons why this approach is advantageous. First, taxable benefits can easily be made consistent with post-disability potential earnings. If benefits are tax-free, those in higher tax brackets (those without dependants or those with other taxable income) have a lower incentive to work than those in lower tax brackets. The tax-free benefits create disparities in replacement rates and adverse work incentives for some groups. The Wyatt (1978, 280) report on workmen's compensation calculates disposable income before and after disablement. Single individuals with higher earnings receive an increase in income as a result of disablement because benefits are tax-free. This calculation is based only on workmen's compensation and does not include other benefits such as those arising from the Canada Pension Plan.

One solution is to define benefits as a percentage of net income, as is now done in Quebec. Saskatchewan (1976, 61) suggested that benefits replace 80 per cent of disposable income, rather than 75 per cent of gross income. In order to do this the scale of benefits must be varied according to marital status and number of dependants. The Saskatchewan report fails to consider that the marital status and number of dependants of the disabled individual might change. Furthermore, other income is not considered in the calculation. One must conclude that it is far more straightforward for the provinces to convince the federal government to tax workmen's compensation benefits and return the revenue to the provinces. The revenue could be used to raise the level of gross workmen's compensation benefits.

There are significant administrative advantages to the proposed approach. Those for whom employers pay sickness and disability insurance premiums do not have to include this benefit in taxable income. Since most insurance is employer-provided and the number disabled is small compared to the number insured, fewer calculations are required when benefits are taxed. If the employer insures the employees, it is not necessary to impute the value of this coverage for each healthy employee.

The taxable benefits approach does not work as smoothly for benefits received for medical expenses. If the Ontario Health Insurance Plan premiums were tax-deductible and the benefits were taxable, some individuals would have

72 Disability insurance and public policy

tax bills that exceed their net income. Each person would have to insure himself against this tax liability arising from illness.

For consistency, individually financed disability insurance should also be made tax-deductible. At present, employee-financed plans provide tax-free benefits, but the premiums do not qualify as a tax deduction. Administrative costs for the government will be higher if individual plans are tax-deductible, but insurance coverage is likely to be more complete because the after-tax ratio of benefits to earnings can be controlled more precisely by the insurance company.

In Chapter 3 it was pointed out that underestimation of risks may lead to under-insurance. One might suspect that if contributions were tax-deductible, insurance coverage would increase because those with incorrect probability perceptions would undervalue the expected tax liability resulting from the taxability of benefits. This turns out not to be the case. The tax-deductibility of premiums and the taxability of benefits have no effect on the insurance decision, regardless of the degree of misperception. Insurance coverage increases in gross terms to offset the tax on benefits, but the after-tax premiums and after-tax benefits remain the same. This conclusion would be altered if the tax-deductibility of premiums increased public awareness of the availability of disability insurance.

Taxes pose a difficult problem when courts attempt to provide the lump-sum equivalent of lost future earnings. Since damages under tort law are supposed to restore the injured victim to the position that he would have enjoyed had he not been injured, the court should provide complete replacement of lost disposable income. If the lost earnings occurred only in the year in which the damages were awarded, the court could simply award the amount of the lost disposable income for that year. When the loss extends into the future, it becomes more difficult to calculate a capital sum that will replace the lost after-tax earnings.

The court's dilemma arises because the recipient will have to invest the capital sum so as to spread his consumption throughout his life. Income from capital will be taxed at a different rate than income from earnings. The dividend and interest exclusion, the dividend tax credit, and the favourable treatment of capital gains are examples of provisions that reduce the taxes on this income compared to taxes on an equal amount of earnings. On the other hand the tax system makes no distinction between nominal and real returns to capital; nominal interest is taxed as if it were real income.

In a recent set of decisions the Supreme Court of Canada (Canada 1978) decided to ignore taxes in awarding compensation for personal injuries. That is, the capital sum would be calculated with gross earnings and a gross rate of return on capital. This approach has the advantage of computational simplicity, but it may bias the results. The Pearson Commission (Great Britain 1978, vol 1, 146)

Disability benefits 73

recommends that the net earnings be capitalized by a net discount rate which equals the after-tax nominal rate of return minus the forecast rate of inflation.[19] This approach would appear to be more precise than that of the Supreme Court, but it ignores the differential taxation of income from capital and the tax-free consumption of capital.

In order to analyse the effects of the alternative approaches, a computer simulation model was devised. The model computes the taxes on the income from a capital sum and iterates to find a constant level of real consumption that can be maintained throughout an individual's life. A level of inflation is assumed that is consistent with the nominal return on capital. It is assumed that earnings will rise by the rate of inflation. Consequently, current dollar earnings can be capitalized using the real rate of return. This result would be nearly the same if the lost earnings were inflated by the expected rate of inflation and the series discounted using a nominal rate of return which equals the real rate of return plus the expected rate of inflation. Table 3 presents the results of six simulations. It turns out that a victim with thirty years' lost earnings will be almost exactly compensated by a sum that was calculated using gross earnings. That is, the capitalized value of $15 000 at a 3 per cent real rate of return generates annual real consumption equal to $12 624, which is nearly equal to disposable income that would have been available after taxes were paid on $15 000 in earnings ($12 584). However, for a shorter work life the victim is overcompensated (18 per cent more consumption for a ten-year life). He is undercompensated over a longer period (14 per cent undercompensated for fifty years). The disparities tend to be greater at higher earnings levels, as shown by the $30 000 case. Furthermore, the higher the rate of inflation, the lower the level of consumption that can be sustained with a lump-sum award because taxes are based on nominal not real income. The after-tax real yield also varies with number of years and the rate of inflation. The last column of Table 3 indicates that the Pearson Commission approach is incorrect for this example. For the $30 000 case their approach would suggest a real after-tax discount rate of $10(1 - 0.27) - 7 = 0.3$, where 0.27 is the average tax rate on $30 000 of earnings. The actual yields are higher than this figure.

One can conclude that the Supreme Court's approach is correct only as a first approximation and introduces biases that depend on the rate of inflation, the amount of earnings, and the length of the period. It would be desirable to refine the calculations with the aid of a computer simulation, but it might be difficult to do this in an adversarial framework. Alternatively, it might be desirable to

---

19 They also subtract the real rate of growth of earnings. This allows for an increase in benefits in real terms along with average earnings in the economy.

TABLE 3

The effects of ignoring taxes in capitalization of lost earnings

Earnings		Capitalized gross earnings	Working life (years)	Annual consumption after award 1977 prices	Percentage increase in consumption	After-tax real yield
Before tax	After tax					
		127 954	10	14 792	+18	2.73
15 000	12 584	294 006	30	12 624	0	1.72
		385 946	50	10 781	−14	1.40
		255 908	10	28 536	+31	2.03
30 000	21 855	588 012	30	22 337	+2	0.86
		771 892	50	17 634	−19	0.82

NOTE: 1977 taxes for a married victim without children; gross earnings are capitalized at 3 per cent.

The award is assumed to be invested 50 per cent in stocks and 50 per cent in bonds. Interest rates are 10 per cent a year, dividends are 5 per cent, capital gains are 5 per cent, and inflation is 7 per cent. The victim is assumed to reinvest a portion of his income in order to maintain constant annual consumption.

introduce new legislation that would permit an expert hired by the court to make damage calculations.

INTEGRATION OF DISABILITY PROGRAMS

The proliferation of disability insurance programs in Canada can prevent the benefit system from achieving the goals of administrative efficiency, optimal insurance, optimal safety, and horizontal equity. The duplication of administrative effort is an obvious inefficiency. The total package of programs may also conflict with the optimal insurance objective. In this chapter it was pointed out that an optimal disability benefit package would contain a waiting period and coverage below 100 per cent of market wages. When all the programs are taken together, the waiting period may effectively be eliminated. For instance, sick leave and unemployment insurance sickness benefits may cover the period between the onset of a disability and the beginning of long-term disability benefits such as the CPP, which has a three-month waiting period. Since the total benefits are determined by the sum of the programs, total benefits may exceed earnings, particularly on an after-tax basis.

Excessive insurance imposes real costs because of the work disincentive effects and the inappropriate division of income between the disabled and healthy states of the world. The overinsurance also creates inequities because

Disability benefits 75

some individuals are eligible for more programs than others. Those who are overinsured would prefer lower levels of contributions and lower levels of coverage. If benefits under one program cause other benefits to fall, those eligible for both are overcontributing compared to those eligible for only one program.

Integration of programs is difficult to achieve because each program affects the other. If private plans supplement workmen's compensation, the number of workmen's compensation claims goes up. If workmen's compensation benefits increase for reasons other than inflation, private insurance companies will profit on previously established disability pensions. Following such a change, premiums will adjust to the new level of supplementary benefits, but the integration forces the private company to bear the risk of changes in public benefits. Purchasers of disability insurance will, in turn, pay a premium to cover this risk. If private insurance benefits are deducted from workmen's compensation benefits, there is an implicit tax on voluntary disability insurance. Such a tax is likely to discourage purchases of supplements to workmen's compensation for all but those with very high levels of desired insurance coverage.

Conflicts between public programs are even less straightforward. Should the CPP benefits be deducted from workmen's compensation benefits or vice versa? The Wyatt (1978) report suggests that workmen's compensation benefits should supplement the CPP benefits, but there is no obvious reason to choose between the two approaches other than administrative efficiency. The applicant's costs will be lower if he only deals with one agency. Administrative costs will be lower if there is only one agency, but this may not be possible unless the eligibility rules are made consistent. The difficult problem of integrating the diverse Canadian programs is discussed in more detail in Chapter 6.

CONCLUSION

This chapter has considered a number of issues related to the design of the disability benefit. Perhaps the most severe obstacle to adequate disability insurance is the difficulty in measuring disability. Most definitions will induce those with impairments to alter their work activity. This response adds to the cost of insurance and forces those who purchase insurance to give up some risk reduction in favour of reduced premiums. A public program faces the same dilemma, but the tradeoffs are usually considered from other points of view. Nevertheless, public programs must be designed as if they were private programs or risk failing to achieve any social objective.

Another critical issue is the choice of lump-sum versus periodic contingent payments. This issue is frequently raised in conjunction with tort compensation, but it is just as relevant for other forms of insurance or compensation. The

76 Disability insurance and public policy

analysis suggests that the argument for periodic payments is much weaker than is believed by many commentators on the legal system. The analysis of the two approaches boils down to a discussion of whether mandatory insurance, in the form of periodic contingent payments, is justified for those already impaired. As pointed out in Chapter 3, the case for mandatory insurance is weak.

Without some adjustment for inflation, the real value of disability benefits will fall continuously. Saving can be used to smooth out consumption, but this only illustrates the low level of long-term consumption that can be sustained by a constant nominal benefit. Public programs such as workmen's compensation can be indexed immediately, but indexation of private benefits will require a more innovative form of government intervention.

Finally, the tax treatment of disability benefits was found to inhibit a rational choice of benefit level. In order to rationalize the system, all benefits, including workmen's compensation, should be taxable, but the premiums should be deductible. The effect of taxes on lump-sum awards is more complicated, but the current approach for non-fatal tort cases is a better approximation to the ideal approach than one would expect.

5
Administrative issues

INTRODUCTION

In a world of perfect information and zero transactions costs the provision of optimal disability insurance and an efficient level of precautions would be a simple task. When information is less than perfect, whether the information concerns precautions or the level of disability, the program design becomes more complex. This chapter considers some of the administrative issues that arise because of imperfect information. For example, does the cost of acquiring information on the specific extent of disability justify the efficiency and equity gains? Is the cost of determining the level of precautions (fault) justified? What types of insurance rate classification should be allowed?

Moral hazard offers one explanation for the proliferation of disability programs. Those activities, groups, or disabilities least likely to be affected by moral hazard are most likely to be covered by insurance programs. However, the separate programs create another problem: how do we determine the boundaries of each specific program? Are the costs of determining those boundaries greater than the advantages of compartmentalizing the insurance coverage? Would a government insurance carrier operating as a monopoly be more efficient than a competitive insurance industry? These questions will be considered in this chapter in light of some general economic principles.

THE DISABILITY DETERMINATION PROCESS

Programs designed to provide benefits only for those considered to be disabled must have some method of determining disability. This method must inevitably produce errors in measurement. These errors result from difficulties in assessing the extent of certain types of impairment and the difficulty in determining the

78 Disability insurance and public policy

effect of a given impairment on economic loss. Although the *expected* estimate of disability may equal the actual disability, an unbiased measurement of disability is of little consolation to those who are denied benefits because their measured disabilities, as opposed to their actual disabilities, happen to fall below the level required for benefits. The benefits not paid to this group will be paid to those whose measured, as opposed to actual, disabilities exceed the minimum.

The errors have several adverse effects on the insurance program. First, the randomness of benefits reduces the effective insurance coverage. If benefits are sufficiently random for some types of disabilities, the coverage will not be purchased. Second, there is a substantial incentive for the disabled person to incur costs that will increase the chances of being judged disabled. Third, the horizontal inequities that result from an error-prone process are likely to cause substantial distrust of the program as a whole. The resulting 'horror stories' are reported in the media to support either the view that deserving individuals are being denied the insurance benefits or the view that the program is too generous.

The variance in the disability determination can be reduced by investment in information. The administrators can undertake more thorough investigation and can provide more appeals procedures. The claimant may also be allowed to retain professional counsel to handle the application. Unfortunately, the latter step may raise the expected measured disability as well as reduce the variance. This shift, in turn, raises the information cost of administrators who attempt to make the procedure unbiased. The resulting escalation of costs may outweigh the benefits of the reduced variance.

One of the ways of reducing the size of the error in each individual case is to vary the benefits with the extent of disability. This can be accomplished by paying a fraction of a full benefit depending on the degree of disability. Another approach is to base benefits on the reduction in earnings, regardless of disability. Both approaches reduce the incentives for marginal cases to incur costs that increase their chances of receiving benefits, but the number of recipients is likely to increase substantially. The fractional-disability approach may result in errors that are large if the fraction of disability does not match the economic loss.

Nagi (1969) analyses the disability-determination process under the U.S. social security system. Comparing a comprehensive clinical evaluation of applicants with the legal determination of disability, he found that 27 per cent of those who could not work competitively were deprived benefits and 37 per cent of those who could work were allowed benefits (ibid. 96). Predictably, the administrative process tended to rely more on readily observable physical disabilities than on psychological disabilities (ibid. 105).

Another dimension of the disability determination process is whether benefits are individually determined or based on more universal formulas or schedules. The supposed advantage of the tort system, in contrast to most social security programs, is that it determines losses, and therefore compensation, on an individual basis. One can be sceptical about this type of argument. Precedents tend to standardize awards regardless of circumstances. On the other hand, the idiosyncracies of judges and juries and their prejudices may make the award a random variable as far as an individual victim is concerned, even after the defendant's negligence has been determined. Uncertainty over future pecuniary losses and reductions for the plaintiff's negligence introduce further gaps between the actual loss and the compensation. Courts may also be poor institutions for making these benefit calculations. In recent Supreme Court cases, as we have seen, a real discount rate of 7 per cent was used to capitalize future losses when 3 per cent would have been more appropriate. The court's confusion over real and nominal interest rates deprived the plaintiffs in these cases of nearly half their benefits.[1] Evidence on the size of loss relative to compensation (Conrad 1964, Ison 1967, Linden 1965, Great Britain 1978) supports the view that individual determination of losses is a worthy objective that is not achieved by the tort system.

The absolute administrative costs are likely to rise with the level of the benefit in response to attempts by the claimant and the payers to acquire more information. The costs will also rise when more specific information is acquired, such as detailed medical evidence or fault. Table 4 presents the ratio of administrative costs to compensation in the United Kingdom. The costs of tort compensation are considerably higher than the costs of alternative systems because of the detailed information and high-priced professionals who are retained by both plaintiff and defendant. The cost of personal accident insurance is high in part because of selling costs (Lees and Doherty 1973, 23).

The extensive administrative costs of the tort compensation system have led critics to suggest that the system is a failure. This view shows a misunderstanding of one of the primary functions of the fault-based system, that is, to promote economic efficiency. This point will be considered in the next section, followed by an examination of no-fault alternatives to fault-based tort compensation.

FAULT-BASED COMPENSATION

Under the common law, courts ordinarily award compensation when the defendant is found to be negligent, in other words to be at fault. The definition of fault that appeals to economists was introduced by Judge Learned Hand. Under the Learned Hand rule the defendant is guilty of negligence if the loss caused by the accident multiplied by the probability of the accident exceeds the cost of avoiding

---

1 For example, in *Arnold* v. *Teno*, [1978] S.C.R., 287, the use of a 7 per cent discount rate as opposed to a 3 per cent rate reduced compensation for future medical costs by 46 per cent.

TABLE 4

Ratio of administrative costs to compensation, United Kingdom (percentage)

Tort	74
Social security	7
Industrial injury and disability	15
Life insurance	15
Personal accident insurance	55
Sick pay	5

SOURCE: Lees and Doherty (1973, 23)

the accident. If negligent, the defendant must compensate the victim for his entire loss including an estimate of non-pecuniary losses, often called pain and suffering. In most circumstances the Learned Hand test, if properly applied, guarantees that an efficient level of precautions will be undertaken (Posner 1977, Brown 1973, Diamond 1974, Calabresi 1970, Schwartz 1978).

The tort method of compensation has the advantage of providing a very complete analysis of the causes and consequences of individual accidents. The court decisions provide signals to actors in the economy to maintain an appropriate standard of care. The implications of the decisions are felt far beyond the courtroom. The tort system relies on the evaluation of precautions after an accident occurs to provide incentives rather than an evaluation of precautions before the accident. This approach has obvious administrative advantages because only a small proportion of all activities are subject to rigorous scrutiny (Wittman 1977). Efficient behaviour is induced because those not undertaking efficient precautions bear the full cost of their actions.

The ideal world of tort law is seldom realized because most potential tortfeasors, whether they be manufacturers, drivers, doctors, or homeowners, etc., are risk-averse and insure against potential tort liability. Once everyone is insured against tort liability there is no incentive to undertake precautions unless the insurance premiums are linked to the level of precautions. Such a link is impractical because the monitoring cost is too high and because we do not usually have sufficient knowledge of the efficacy of precautions. Furthermore, if the insurance premiums are raised by the full amount of the award after a successful tort claim against the insurance company, the insurance protection is effectively eliminated. Insurance companies can only make crude adjustments in rates, with some adjustment if there have been previous claims. This adjustment is called experience rating.

If tortfeasors are fully insured, the only deterrent effect of the fault-based tort system is the added insurance premium that will be assessed following

Administrative issues 81

determination of negligence. These added premiums may exceed the tort liability for small losses but on average will be much less than the actual loss. Consequently, the determination of fault is of interest mainly to the insurance company defending against the claim. Nevertheless, Grayston (1973) found some evidence that insurance rates can affect the accident rate.

NO-FAULT PROGRAMS

Unfortunately, the elaborate information-gathering process in tort cases is an extremely costly way of delivering compensation, and by definition only a fraction of those injured, the victims of accidents demonstrably caused by someone else's negligence, will receive compensation. Furthermore, widespread insurance coverage mitigates the incentives for efficient precautions against accidents. As these defects have become more widely appreciated, the no-fault approach has been introduced in many jurisdictions in North America. Workmen's compensation is the first example of this approach, and more recently the no-fault approach has been extended to those injured in automobile accidents. Saskatchewan, Manitoba, Ontario, and Alberta have partial no-fault personal injury coverage, but Quebec is the only jurisdiction in which no-fault compensation for personal injuries resulting from automobile accidents has completely replaced the injured person's right to take legal action against a negligent driver.

No-fault automobile insurance for personal injuries as generally proposed is really a combination of many changes in the existing system. First, it eliminates an automobile driver's liability for losses suffered by those in another automobile. Second, it imposes mandatory disability insurance on all drivers. Third, it imposes strict liability on drivers for the losses of passengers and pedestrians. Fourth, it imposes liability insurance on all drivers to cover the losses of passengers and pedestrians. Fifth, it reduces the level of benefits paid compared to fault-based compensation. And sixth, the benefits are periodic rather than lump-sum. These six changes constitute the so-called no-fault approach.

Obviously each of the six changes could be introduced independently. For example, there is no necessary connection between the choice of a fault system and the choice between lump-sum and periodic compensation. In many countries fault systems are combined with periodic compensation. Conversely, no-fault systems can award lump-sum payments. It is clear, however, that the courts are likely to be poor administrators of periodic contingent payments and defendants as a whole are likely to be unsatisfactory guarantors of periodic payments. If mandatory periodic payments are seen as desirable within a fault system, notwithstanding the arguments made in Chapter 4, insurance companies or institutions such as the Workmen's Compensation Board would be more efficient

82 Disability insurance and public policy

administrators of periodic payments. Lump-sum awards could be paid by the defendant to the administrator (and insurer) of the periodic payment.

One could also imagine that the liability of drivers for injury to other drivers could be eliminated without imposing mandatory disability insurance. In Chapter 3 the case for mandatory insurance was found to be weak. The argument for mandatory liability insurance against the claims of pedestrians and passengers is somewhat different. Although the pedestrians and passengers could always insure themselves, mandatory insurance for the driver will be more likely to guarantee that drivers as a whole, if not individual drivers, bear the cost of accidents to pedestrians and passengers. In the absence of mandatory insurance 'judgment-proof' drivers would not bear any cost. In the absence of insurance, the strict liability of drivers for accidents to pedestrians and passengers would induce efficient precautions if the pedestrian did not contribute to the probability of an accident. Since pedestrians bear some of the cost of accidents under no-fault proposals because of the lack of compensation for pain and suffering, they have an incentive to avoid accidents. On balance, strict liability of drivers for injuries to non-drivers coupled with mandatory liability insurance appears to be justifiable on the grounds that drivers can best avoid accidents and that variations in their insurance rates will offer some incentive to do so.

The appropriate level of benefits will be lower under a no-fault program or any other program in which each person insures himself. The optimal insurance will compensate only for pecuniary loss (as long as the marginal utility of income at a given income level is not changed). In theory, tort damages compensate for the entire loss of utility. Advocates of no-fault programs suggest that compensation levels be lower than under tort law on the grounds that more people are compensated under no-fault programs. Their conclusions are justified by the insurance model. However, if pedestrians and passengers cannot affect the probability of an accident, they should be compensated for their entire loss in order to induce drivers to take appropriate precautions and make them pay for the entire social cost of their activity.

The no-fault proposals often contain some element of fault determination. In effect they retain what little incentive exists as a result of experience rating and deductibles. Under many so-called no-fault schemes, such as that proposed by the Ontario (1978) Select Committee, each person is compensated by his own insurance company in case of accident, but he may be able to collect the deductible portion (for property damage) if the other party involved in the accident is found to be at fault. Similarly, the party at fault might be charged with an additional premium on future insurance coverage. A no-fault scheme with these provisions offers a very modest incentive to undertake precautions, but it retains a simplified fault-determination process, where the stakes are greatly reduced from the tort process. A tort case may involve the potential loss of $1 million by the insurance company and the possibility that the plaintiff will either collect that amount or remain uncompensated. With stakes this large the process must be very thorough and allow for appeals, postponements, and other procedures for reducing errors. In contrast, the social costs of errors resulting from an incorrect assessment of the deductible or a revision of the insurance rate are relatively small. The procedures for allocating fault in such cases do not have to be nearly as formal or costly.

Saskatchewan and Manitoba have provisions for placing a surcharge on the insurance premium for those who are 50 per cent or more at fault. The fault determination is made by insurance adjusters subject to appeal to the Small Claims Court (Saskatchewan) or the Rates Appeal Board (Manitoba). In both cases the surcharges are relatively small ($25 in Saskatchewan) and last for only one year. It is questionable whether there is any perceptible deterrent effect from such small penalties. Traffic fines and a possible loss of a driver's licence will present a much greater incentive for caution.

In conclusion, at least two important features of the no-fault system are not well appreciated. First, no-fault programs impose mandatory disability insurance. This feature may not be desirable. Second, the fault-determination process remains, but the stakes involved are greatly reduced. Fault determination under many so-called no-fault schemes involves merely a determination of insurance rates. Consequently the cost of errors is reduced and the process can be simplified. A greater possibility of errors in fault determination reduces the incentive to take precautions, but this effect will most likely be small. If this simplified fault determination does not induce enough alteration of behaviour to justify its cost, a true no-fault program in which experience does not enter the insurance rate classification may be desirable.

SPECIFIC VERSUS UNIVERSAL PROGRAMS

There are at least three explanations for the present system of disability programs, where coverage differs greatly depending on the type of accident and the type of disability. First, some of the programs are designed to redistribute income from all taxpayers to particular classes of individuals. Specific programs for the blind or those suffering from criminal injuries are examples of this type of program. Second, some programs are motivated by a desire to force particular individuals, groups, or institutions to bear the cost of certain disabilities. Workmen's compensation is incorrectly believed to force employers to bear the cost of industrial injuries. The common law forces (uninsured) negligent defendants to bear the cost of disability suffered by non-negligent plaintiffs.[2] Third, programs are limited because moral hazard is too great if the programs are extended to other groups, other sources of disability, or other types of disability. These three explanations for the wide variety of present programs will be discussed in turn.

Programs designed to assist a certain narrow segment of the disabled are hard to justify if we recognize that the economic consequences of a disability are not necessarily related to the cause or the type of disability. If the objective is to provide insurance against all disabilities, a universal program with uniform coverage for all is preferable. Such a program eliminates duplication of administrative expense and costly determination of eligibility.

The universal approach is subject to the criticism that it may not allocate the social cost of risky activities to those able to take precautions and affect the extent of those activities. Ideally, insurance rates are based on the precautions of individuals or firms in order to induce optimal precautions. Since this is rarely the case in practice, the best that can be hoped for is that broad classes of drivers or industries bear the cost of their activity. This does not produce the optimal level of safety that would prevail if there were perfect information, but it allows potential drivers, for instance, to weigh the costs and benefits of driving (the insurance premium) against those of other modes of transportation. As mentioned above, Grayston (1973) found some evidence that insurance rates affect the number of automobile registrations. Similarly, a higher workmen's compensation assessment on firms in a risky industry will not induce each firm to take the ideal level of precautions, but it will induce substitution that reduces the number of accidents, compared to a situation in which assessments are uniform across all industries. Higher levels of workmen's compensation assessments in risky industries will induce firms in those industries to substitute capital for labour and induce consumers of the products to substitute towards goods produced using safer techniques.

The advantages of this cost allocation must be weighed against the cost of determining the cause of a particular disability. The history of workmen's compensation is filled with legal disputes over whether a particular accident is work-related. The same problems occur when there are two competing insurance programs. For example, if there are separate funds for automoboile injuries and work injuries, the cost of a particular automobile accident involving business activity must be apportioned to them. If a consumer is injured, it must be

---

2 Under Ontario's comparative negligence regime the negligent plaintiff will bear a portion of the cost of the accident.

determined whether use of a particular product caused the accident, and perhaps whether the consumer misused the product. No data exist on the administrative costs of allocating accidents to particular industries, products, or activities, but such costs may be small in relation to the efficiency gains achieved. A program with universal coverage could still achieve these efficiencies if it were financed with differential assessments on different activities.

The final reason for activity-specific or disability-specific as opposed to universal programs is moral hazard. The moral hazard may arise because of the effect of insurance on precaution and on the size of the measured loss. As pointed out in Chapter 3, insurance against work-related injuries will be more readily provided by employers than insurance against all injuries because the employer can take precautionary measures and can monitor employee precautions. One reason why programs for the blind developed early is that blindness can be determined more objectively than many other disabilities. Mental disorders are often excluded from private insurance contracts because of the difficulty of monitoring the severity of the disorder. Self-employed individuals may be excluded from insurance coverage because of the difficulty of measuring the size of the loss.[3]

The most obvious division in the programs is between those working in the market place and those working in the home. The latter are not eligible for public programs such as workmen's compensation, unemployment insurance, sickness benefits, or the Canada Pension Plan. One explanation for the exclusion of those involved in household production is that the amount of insurable (pecuniary) loss is likely to be smaller than the loss suffered by a wage-earner and certainly harder to measure. A disability may lower the quantity and quality of household production but does not produce a measurable loss unless the household services are replaced in the marketplace. Despite their thorough investigation of losses, courts have had difficulty determining the loss resulting from a housewife's disability.[4] Consequently, the moral hazard problem is likely to be severe for non-market workers.

Although moral hazard may suggest reduced coverage for certain activities or disabilities, there is a serious problem of equity in such an approach. The disabled person who is not provided benefits because of the difficulty of proving the extent of disability is likely to feel unjustly treated when he observes others

---

3 Palmer (1977) reports that the self-employed have presented problems in the early years of the New Zealand compensation program.
4 In one disability case an Ontario court evaluated the loss of a housewife's services at $5000 a year, the cost of hiring a housekeeper. *Franco et al.* v. *Woolfe et al.* 52 D.L.R. (3rd), 355.

86 Disability insurance and public policy

with similar disabilities receiving public benefits. This problem does not occur with a voluntary private program because the insurance purchaser is assumed to know the terms of his coverage. On the other hand a universal public program that compensates those whose disabilities are subject to moral hazard will appear to be inequitable to those who pay taxes and do not claim benefits.

In conclusion, administrative efficiency is the primary justification for a universal program. In the absence of administrative costs the efficiency criterion suggests that programs should be designed to assign the costs of accidents to the activities, if not the individuals, that are responsible for accidents. Moral hazard also suggests that differential coverage for different types of accidents and disabilities may be optimal. Some of the administrative advantages of completely universal programs can be achieved by combining all coverage under one administrative entity without making premiums and coverage equal for all types of accidents and disabilities.

PUBLIC VERSUS PRIVATE PROVISION OF INSURANCE

Given the public provision of automobile insurance in British Columbia, Saskatchewan, and Manitoba, the advantages and the disadvantages of publicly provided insurance must be considered for Ontario. This issue is distinct from the other dimensions of a compensation system such as mandatory versus voluntary coverage or fault versus no-fault compensation. In western Canada an argument was made that 'if all members of the motoring public are compelled to buy insurance, they should not therefore be compelled to contribute to private sector profits' (Ontario 1978, 97). On this argument the clothing industry should be nationalized because the law requires people to wear clothes in public. In the United States a substantial portion of workmen's compensation is handled through private insurance carriers, while Ontario administers workmen's compensation through a government agency.

Economic theory suggests that in certain conditions competitive industries will lead to a more efficient allocation of resources than a regulated monopoly or a government-run monopoly. The primary reason for the theoretical superiority of the competitive system is that the prices of products, prices of factors of production, and profits become signals for the individual agents in the system to act efficiently. Ideally, a government industry could achieve exactly the same result, but in practice this may not be possible because of the difficulty in motivating and directing the managers and workers of a government monopoly to act efficiently. The inefficiency of the non-competitive firm is most likely to show up in the long run as the firm fails to respond to changing technology

Administrative issues 87

and market conditions and as the internal structure becomes more rigid. In a competitive industry new firms with new ideas force other firms to overcome their own inertia and adapt to changing conditions or risk going out of business.

On the other hand, imperfect information, which makes it difficult to duplicate the competitive outcome in a regulated or government-run firm, also raises the costs of a competitive system. Competitive firms must devote substantial resources to advertising and selling their products and consumers must bear the cost of searching for the most favourable product and price. It is an empirical question whether the efficiency advantages of a competitive industry outweigh these additional costs. In one study related to the insurance industry Frech (1976) found that non-profit firms had higher costs in processing health claims.

Public operation of automobile insurance was carefully considered by the Ontario Select Committee on Company Law (Ontario 1978) but ultimately rejected. The primary argument in favour of a public insurance carrier is that administrative costs may be lower under a monopoly insurance company. Cost savings could occur because of the economies of scale, lower selling costs, and the elimination of disputes between insurance companies. An analysis of the cost of insurance in Manitoba, Saskatchewan, and British Columbia indicates that automobile insurance rates are substantially lower than in Ontario (Ontario 1978; Kennedy and Mehr 1977). However, direct comparison is difficult because of the significant subsidization of urban policy holders by rural policy holders in Manitoba and Saskatchewan (Ontario 1978, 408). Furthermore, one must consider other factors which might account for differences in rates, such as accident frequency. Another approach is to examine the administrative costs as a percentage of total expenditures. Manitoba and Saskatchewan spend about 83 per cent of expenditures on claims, compared to 76 per cent for British Columbia and 64 per cent for Ontario (Ontario 1978, 94). The difference in the percentage of administrative costs would be meaningless if the total claims were substantially different between the provinces, but the Ontario Select Committee found no evidence of this.

Half of the apparent difference in costs arises because of lower acquisition costs for the government insurance system (Ontario 1978, 436). A competitive market imposes higher information-gathering costs because consumers must be made aware of the alternative price and quantity available in the market place. Consumers also bear search costs when shopping for policies. These costs may be lowered if the range of policies available to the consumer is narrowed. The costs are further reduced if there is only one company and one price per type of policy. On the other hand the added costs in the competitive market may be more than offset by the benefits of the wider choice that is available.

The other half of the gap between the costs arises from claims processing costs. The lower cost of the government monopoly are likely to result from

88 Disability insurance and public policy

elimination of intercompany disputes over fault and damages. However, these same cost savings can be realized by a private no-fault program. Manitoba and Saskatchewan have a compulsory collision coverage system that eliminates disputes over fault for all but the deductible portion of the damages. There is little incentive on the part of drivers or the insurance carrier to invest substantial resources in determining fault because the amounts are relatively small. In both Saskatchewan and Manitoba insurance adjusters decide on fault in order to assess surcharges on drivers found to be 50 per cent or more at fault. This fault-determination process is likely to be considerably less extensive than the intercompany negotiations that arise in Ontario. In Florida the partial introduction of no-fault property damage resulted in a 9 per cent increase in the benefit/premium ratio according to one study (Widiss et al. 1977, 325).

Although Manitoba, Saskatchewan and British Columbia have fault-based personal injury benefits (in addition to no-fault disability benefits, referred to as 'accident benefits'), the amount of litigation is significantly lower than Ontario's. In Ontario the number of lawsuits per vehicle is 2.5 times the number in Manitoba, Saskatchewan, and British Columbia (Ontario 1978, 399). A lower level of litigation and corresponding cost savings could be achieved in Ontario with more significant no-fault coverage whether or not there is public provision of insurance. In Florida the introduction of limited no-fault coverage for personal injuries (tort liability was eliminated only for small claims) increased the benefit/premium ratio by 56 per cent (Widiss et al. 1977, 313).

Another argument for public provision of insurance is the inability of private insurance companies to offer indexed benefits (see Chapter 4). Public companies are safe from bankruptcy caused by unanticipated inflation because they have the ability to fall back on tax revenues. Over long periods there should be no net cost resulting from unanticipated inflation because the positive and negative unanticipated inflation should cancel out. However, there are other methods of providing indexed benefits within a competitive system, such as sale of indexed bonds to insurance companies or government insurance of real returns. Since one of these approaches may be taken in conjunction with private retirement pensions, there may be no need to move towards public insurance solely because of the inflation problem.

A similar problem occurs if there are other states of the world which increase the liabilities of private insurance companies but not their assets. For instance, a general depression might lower the value of an insurance company's portfolio but increase the number of beneficiaries because unemployment raises disability benefit applications. A government insurance scheme could also be devised to cover this contingency without introducing government disability insurance.

Administrative issues 89

In summary it appears that many of the cost advantages of a public insurance carrier could be duplicated with a no-fault system. Another major portion of the differences can be accounted for by selling costs that may or may not be equalled by the benefits that consumers enjoy from a wider selection of companies with which to deal and a wider choice of policies. A public system can more easily affect cross-subsidization between risk groups (see below), but a monopoly public insurance carrier has no economic incentive for development of rates that more closely approximate risks. Furthermore, in the design of the benefit structure and the administration of benefits a public system is extremely sensitive to political pressures that ultimately may make the system less efficient than a private system.

RISK CLASSIFICATION AND STATISTICAL DISCRIMINATION

One of the other attributes of public programs is that the rate classification system is usually much simpler than under a private system. Insurance companies attempt to divide the insured population into classes based on the probability of accident. There is an economic incentive for each company in a private system to devise finer breakdowns in order to attract low-risk customers from other firms. The number of classifications will therefore expand whenever there is sufficient information to justify an additional classification. This process is limited by the cost of acquiring detailed information and the lack of information relating personal characteristics to the risk of accidents.

The standard approach can lead to extensive inequities in premiums because our knowledge of the personal characteristics that lead to accidents is limited. Rate classifications must be based on easily determined characteristics such as age, sex, marital status, type of automobile, locality, and the amount of insurance purchased. A recent case before the Alberta Human Rights Commission illustrates the problems that arise when characteristics such as sex are used to indicate risk. In this case a female annuitant claimed that she was discriminated against because she was implicitly charged a higher price for a life annuity than a man, and the Borad of Inquiry supported her position. Figure 11 shows the frequency distribution of cost per dollar of life annuity for an annuity purchased at age 65 with an 8 per cent interest rate.[5] Since a life annuity is basically

---

5 This distribution is calculated from general life tables (Canada 1974) and is not necessarily representative of the mortality of annuitants. It is assumed that the annuity is purchased on the sixty-fifth birthday, with annuity payments made at the end of each year. No administrative costs are included.

90 Disability insurance and public policy

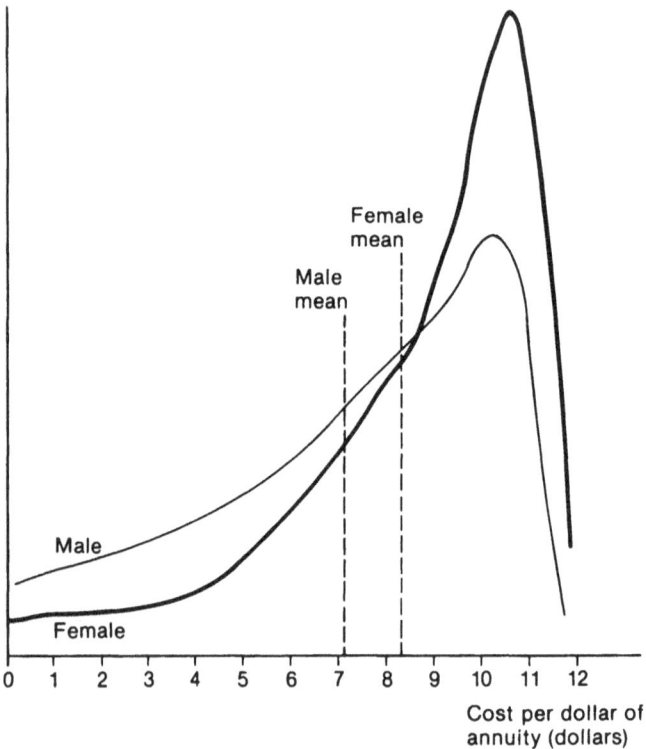

Figure 11: Frequency distribution of life annuity cost, annuity commencing at age 65, 8 per cent interest

insurance against outliving one's financial resources, the cost to the insurance company increases with longevity. In the example the mean cost is 17 per cent higher for women than men because of their greater life expectancy. In spite of the higher average cost for women, there is substantial overlap between the two groups. If women are charged 17 per cent more than men, 65 per cent of the women (the area under both curves) will pay more than men who die at the same age. This group can be said to be victims of statistical discrimination; that is, they pay more for life annuities because some women live longer than men.

If existing indicators of risk are not permitted, there will be changes in the quantities of insurance purchased. For instance, if differential rates for men and women are not permitted, the price of life annuities for men will rise and the price will fall for women. This will induce more women to buy annuities and induce men to reduce their purchases. The price must rise even further as the proportion of women rises. It is possible in some situations that the price increase would deter all low-risk individuals from buying insurance. If this occurs the economic costs would be substantial, and the high-risk group would gain nothing. In the less extreme case of mandatory risk-pooling, inefficiencies will result not only because of the distortion of the insurance decision but also because the high-risk group will overconsume the activity being insured while the low-risk group will underconsume. For instance, if high-risk drivers are subsidized, there will be excessive driving by high-risk drivers.

Statistical discrimination is a problem in other areas of economic life. Non-whites and women are often denied job opportunities because employers base estimates of productivity on the (perceived) productivity of other non-whites or women. This occurs because individuals have no way of signalling their own individual productivity. Similarly, a low-risk driver falling in a high-risk classification has no way of convincing an insurance company that he is not typical of his group. Is there something unjust about this type of discrimination? If relevant information on risk is ignored, inequities defined as the difference between premiums and expected loss will be increased. However, society may feel that distinctions made on certain characteristics such as race or 'life style' are unjust.

A public insurance system is not under competitive pressure to match premiums to losses. It can force subsidization of one group by another. For instances, in Manitoba and Saskatchewan rural drivers subsidize urban drivers, and younger drivers do not pay as great a penalty as in Ontario. This is sometimes seen as a desirable attribute of a public system, but these cost subsidies can be achieved by regulation of the classifications that can be used by the private sector. Classifications based on characteristics such as sex can be prohibited, and private companies can be forced to provide coverage to all customers regardless of personal characteristics. However, private companies can always discourage customers who they feel are bad risks in subtle ways that are unlikely to be detected by the regulators. It may prove costly to require that private insurance companies maintain a system of cross-subsidization. On the other hand, it is not obvious that the classifications now used in Ontario are generally viewed as unfair. Discrimination based on age, sex, and marital status is just as prominent in the tax system as in the present automobile insurance classifications.

6
Evaluation of existing programs

In this chapter the existing sources of disability insurance are examined in light of the analysis in the earlier chapters. Since there are several sources of detailed information on these programs (Brown 1977, Wyatt 1978, Ontario 1978, Coward 1977), the discussion will not describe the programs in detail but will analyse their major strengths and weaknesses in light of the insurance model. The analysis of provincial programs focuses on Ontario.

CANADA PENSION PLAN

The Canada Pension Plan provides disability benefits to those who have contributed for at least five years and have met other requirements concerning the number of years of contribution. The disability benefits are related to past earnings but are subject to a maximum that in 1978 was $2328. Unlike programs such as workmen's compensation, the cause of disability is not a factor in determining eligibility under the Canada Pension Plan.

The CPP is sometimes criticized for its three-month waiting period (Brown 1977, 314), but such a provision is an important feature of an insurance scheme subject to moral hazard. The low levels of benefits can be more validly criticized. The CPP does not provide sufficient income for those without other sources of coverage, yet it might lead to overcompensation of those who receive other benefits, such as tort compensation or workmen's compensation. No-fault automobile accident benefits in Ontario are reduced by the amount of CPP disability benefits. In some cases welfare benefits fall when CPP benefits are indexed for inflation (Brown 1977, 320). Therefore the degree of insurance depends not only on the CPP but on one's eligibility for other programs.

One important and often overlooked provision of the CPP disability program is that the disabled person in effect accumulates entitlement to a CPP retirement

Evaluation of existing programs 93

pension without making further contributions. The disability provisions implicitly provide an amount each year equal to the contributions that would have been made.[1] This benefit can be of substantial value.

The Canada Pension Plan requires that a disability be severe and prolonged. 'Severe' means that the person is 'incapable regularly of pursuing any substantially gainful occupation.' The Pension Appeals Board decisions indicate the actual interpretation of this definition (CCH Canadian 1978). In practice, skill or education levels are taken into account along with the impairment in determining whether or not the person is capable of working. For example, a Grade 6 education coupled with severe back problems will qualify a claimant for benefits (CCH Canadian 1978, ¶8702), while enrolment in a university program is considered to enhance one's job prospects sufficiently to overcome the loss of a leg (ibid. ¶8682). The importance placed on education as a factor likely to increase the demand for a person's labour is inconsistent with the general principle that 'availability of suitable jobs is not a criterion with which this Board is concerned' (ibid. ¶8746). Despite this type of statement the existence of jobs in the economy for a person of a given skill and impairment has an implicit influence on the definition of disability.

In Chapter 4 it was stated that the Canada Pension Plan could be characterized as a program in which any work at all disqualifies a person from benefits. In the Act, employment is consistent with disability as long as it is not regular, substantial, and gainful. However, when faced with a disability, no matter how severe, the Pension Appeals Board almost always denies the disability benefit if the applicant or recipient does any work, no matter how little ($40-$50 per month, ibid. ¶8638). For example, one recipient was elected alderman for the City of Oshawa, a job with a salary of $3000 a year (ibid. ¶8683). Although his disability had not changed, he was disqualified from further benefits. Enrolment in university may also disqualify an applicant because it indicates an ability to engage in similar work activities (ibid. ¶8719). In many cases employment income on previous income tax returns is sufficient to rule out disability (ibid. ¶8619, 8621, 8697, 8699, 8720). The classic case concerns a man who had lost the use of both legs, one arm, and one eye. He nevertheless managed to farm for many years before applying for disability benefits. The Pension Appeals Board concluded that he was not prevented from engaging in a gainful occupation (ibid. ¶8559). Contrary decisions in which pensions were awarded despite intermittent work activity are rare (ibid. ¶8634, 8745).

---

1 The implicit amount of contributions equals the previous average contribution increased each year by the growth rate of average earnings (or the growth in the year's maximum pensionable earnings).

94 Disability insurance and public policy

The disability test is stringent enough to disqualify someone who is already impaired from working for a token period in order to apply for disability benefits. Having worked in spite of the impairment, he would be considered capable of gainful employment. Therefore, the provisions that require five years' contributions seem unnecessary. A one-year period of contributions would be sufficient to establish that there had been a loss of earnings.

A CPP beneficiary must have made contributions in at least five of the previous ten years. This provision guarantees that the impaired person has recently been in the labour force. The rule is appropriate if there is to be a relationship between disability and loss of income, but it will have to be revised if the number of years of contributions is altered. A rule that a claimant must have contributed at some point in the last two years, with an exception (perhaps one year of contributions out of the last six) for mothers of young children, would accomplish the desired result.

The CPP's strong points are that it offers an indexed benefit and that it provides benefits to those not usually covered by other public programs, such as the self-employed. Its main drawbacks are the severity and all-or-nothing nature of the disability test, the long contribution period, and the overlap with other programs such as workmen's compensation. If the latter program is indexed, some form of integration with workmen's compensation could be accomplished. The integration problem is addressed in the next section.

WORKMEN'S COMPENSATION

The Ontario Workmen's Compensation Board provides temporary benefits equal to 75 per cent of lost earnings (reduced in cases of partial disability) and permanent benefits which are predetermined at the onset of permanent disability. The permanent benefits are either 75 per cent of lost earnings in the case of total disability, or a reduced amount determined by a schedule of partial disability. This schedule may have only a crude relationship to economic loss, but this approach to benefits is efficient from the point of view of work incentives. Once such a benefit is determined, it is not reduced because of future earnings. In this sense workmen's compensation is similar to tort compensation.

The advantage of the current workmen's compensation approach for permanent disability is improved work incentives and low monitoring costs. The disadvantage of the approach is that the benefits might not cover the actual insurable loss. It is interesting to note that most private insurance plans cover total rather than partial disability. In practice it appears that total disability is easier to demonstrate under private plans than under workmen's compensation. The all-or-nothing approach has more severe work disincentives, and it excludes coverage for smaller losses, but it might on balance be preferable to the present Workmen's Compensation Board approach because coverage against total disability is more advantageous for the risk-averse individual than coverage against partial disability. The approach used for temporary disability, in which benefits are related to lost earnings, may be too costly for an insurance company to administer because the company must determine whether the lost earnings are consistent with the extent of disability.

The present workmen's compensation provisions are difficult to reform because of the origins of the system. It was introduced as a no-fault substitute for tort liability of employers and is perceived as a benefit which employers are obliged to provide to employees. However, it is rarely recognized that employees are likely to bear the entire cost of workmen's compensation through decreased wages. Once this is understood, the system can be analysed as an insurance scheme in which benefits to injured employees are paid for by healthy employees. Viewed in this light either reductions or increases in benefits might be worthwhile, depending on the value of the insurance coverage relative to the cost of the coverage. In particular, employees may not wish to be insured against impairments which do not produce any economic loss. For instance, a lost finger, although unfortunate, will not be insured against if it does not affect earnings (and the marginal utility of income).

There are two features of the workmen's compensation benefits that are particularly irrational. First, the benefits are not adjusted for inflation in Ontario; and second, the benefits are not taxable. The lack of indexation in Ontario is inexplicable, because benefits in Quebec and British Columbia are indexed. If the benefits are designed to replace a fraction of forgone earnings, it makes no sense to let the benefit/earnings ratio fall arbitrarily with the rate of inflation. The makeshift adjustments in benefit levels since 1974 have only offset a fraction of the loss of purchasing power for those on permanent pensions. It is true that a person in receipt of a fixed nominal pension can save a fraction of his income in order to have a constant stream of real consumption. But this process is only practical for anticipated inflation. The individual must still bear the risks of unanticipated inflation. Furthermore, the real benefit level, averaged over a lifetime, will be considerably lower than the statutory ratio of benefits to earnings. The costs of indexation in Ontario are calculated in Wyatt (1978).

At the same time the workmen's compensation benefit should be made taxable. The present system provides greater benefits, relative to earnings, to those with other sources of income and no dependants. In some cases disposable income rises after disability. Although inflation eliminates this problem, it makes

96 Disability insurance and public policy

more sense to provide indexation and tax disability benefits so that the replacement rate is consistent across individuals and over time. The extra revenue collected from taxation of benefits could be used in the short run to assist in financing indexation. Without the taxation of benefits the design of a benefit structure which replaces a given fraction of net earnings is excessively complicated. Saskatchewan (1976), Manitoba (1977), and Wyatt (1978) all propose that benefits be determined with reference to net income, as is now done in Quebec. This approach requires that the benefits be altered for any change in taxable income, including an adjustment for the number of months of disability income in a year. This procedure, which is analogous to using the Workmen's Compensation Board as a tax-collecting agency, unnecessarily adds to the complexity of determining workmen's compensation benefits. Similarly, workmen's compensation benefits should be included in income for purposes of the Guaranteed Income Supplement and GAINS-A.

The overlap between workmen's compensation and CPP benefits is of some concern because it creates excessive administrative costs and overinsurance for some groups. One obvious approach would be to merge the two programs, but this would involve either an expansion of workmen's compensation to include non-work accidents or a reduction in CPP coverage. In the absence of such a major change, integration of workmen's compensation with other programs can nevertheless be achieved. The Wyatt (1978) report suggests that virtually all other benefits be deducted from workmen's compensation benefits, including private insurance and the Guaranteed Income Supplement. This would considerably reduce the benefits payable under workmen's compensation, but it is a questionable approach when applied to GIS benefits and private benefits. By making workmen's compensation the payer of last resort, those with incomes low enough to qualify for GIS would in effect be financing their own GIS benefits through workmen's compensation contributions.

The Wyatt approach would effectively eliminate private (including group) insurance coverage for those with desired insurance that is not sufficiently greater than workmen's compensation. For instance, if workmen's compensation paid 75 per cent of earnings and a group were insured for 90 per cent of earnings, the additional coverage might be declined. In order to receive the extra 15 percentage points of coverage, the employees would have to pay for 90 percentage points of coverage in addition to the workmen's compensation assessment. The proposed approach would greatly discourage private insurance coverage. It is suggested in Appendix B that an income-tested benefit for those with illness or disability might have a 100 per cent tax on private benefits in order to minimize disincentives. The difference between that suggestion and the Wyatt proposal is that the guaranteed income is intended to reach those who would not otherwise

Evaluation of existing programs 97

have insurance and whose incomes are low enough that they should not be required to contribute towards a mandatory insurance scheme. The disincentive to insure privately which exists under the income-tested program can be tolerated because the program meets income redistribution objectives. Workmen's compensation, coupled with a tax on private benefits, would produce little redistribution. Private benefits would be chosen, despite the tax, only by those with desired insurance levels greatly in excess of the maximum compensable earnings. This small group would subsidize the others because they would receive no workmen's compensation benefits, but the losses to those who are induced to drop their private insurance would be great.

The choice between the CPP and workmen's compensation as first payers is not particularly important, although any change in the integration rules is always subject to the criticism that benefits cannot be lowered because past contributions created an entitlement to benefits for those not yet disabled. This general argument may be true for retirement persons, but it is inappropriate for insurance. If a driver pays insurance premiums but has no accidents over a long period, this does not imply that an insurance company cannot raise the price of future insurance. Since the CPP disability benefits are relatively low, it might be easiest to deduct them from workmen's compensation benefits, particularly if workmen's compensation becomes indexed. The beneficiary would still accumulate retirement benefits if eligible for a CPP disability pension. For those over 65, the work-incentive effects of disability pensions are relatively unimportant. Therefore, it is not necessary to hold benefits below 100 per cent of earnings, and the most straightforward approach is to allow accumulation of retirement income from all sources without any offsets. Workmen's compensation should affect GIS benefits, but workmen's compensation need not be reduced for other retirement benefits. The disabled pensioner is unlikely to have significantly more income than he would have had without the disability because disability provisions in private pension plans will adjust to the workmen's compensation benefits.

In the absence of a merger of the public programs, the preferred approach to integration for workmen's compensation is to deduct mandatory public benefits such as CPP benefits and unemployment insurance benefits, but only when total public benefits exceed 75 per cent of the compensable earnings (indexed for inflation). Otherwise, those with partial benefits are unable to receive additional compensation should they be considered disabled by the CPP or should they be eligible for unemployment benefits in the future. Supplementary private plans add to the cost of public plans because the resulting benefit package creates greater moral hazard. This problem can be dealt with by raising the assessment an appropriate amount when supplementary group plans exist, or by partially

98 Disability insurance and public policy

offsetting the private benefits. The appropriate tax rate on private supplementary benefits will be much less than the 100 per cent tax suggested in Wyatt (1978).

Workmen's compensation not only provides benefits for the worker; it also insures the employer against fluctuations in the injury rates. Those employees in Schedule 1, which comprises most of private industry, pay an assessment which is based on their industry classification, not their precautions. In order to provide some incentives for safety (other than those that exist through wage differentials that offset losses not compensated by workmen's compensation) there is some experience rating and an additional surcharge for those with poor claims records. The extent of these adjustments is limited and could be greatly expanded, particularly for large employers whose yearly claims are statistically accurate measures of underlying accident probabilities.

AUTOMOBILE NO-FAULT PROVISIONS

In Ontario, automobile insurance companies are required to include no-fault disability benefits, called 'accident benefits,' in every policy. Someone who is employed as of the date of an accident[2] receives 80 per cent of his gross weekly earnings, subject to a maximum of $140 per week,[3] for two years. The benefits will continue beyond that time only if the person is permanently and totally disabled. Housekeepers receive only $70 a week for twelve weeks.

Accident benefits are reduced by the amount of public plans such as the CPP and, effective in 1978, 'wage or salary continuation plans available to the person by reason of his employment.'[4] The distinction between plans provided through employment and plans purchased privately appears to be based on the naive assumption that the employee does not pay for group plans. In effect this mandatory coverage is not available to those who already have group insurance covering 80 per cent or more of lost earnings. The so-called no-fault coverage could best be labelled mandatory 'no coverage' insurance, since it forces all employees to pay for those not covered by group plans. One logical response to this provision would be to eliminate coverage for automobile accidents from group plans. Unfortunately, this reduces the percentage coverage below 80 per cent for those earning more than $180 per week, the earnings at which the

---

2 If not employed but aged between 18 and 65, one must have worked six months out of the preceding twelve.
3 There is also a limitation on total benefits from all sources.
4 The plan includes a reduction of the amount by which the sum of all benefits exceeds the lost earnings.

Evaluation of existing programs 99

accident benefits reach a maximum. Anyone wishing to maintain 80 per cent replacement, or anyone wishing to increase coverage beyond 80 per cent, must pay for private group coverage in addition to paying for accident benefits for those not covered. The design of the accident benefit program discriminates against those who desire to purchase additional private insurance through their employer.

The problem introduced by deducting group benefits from accident benefits can be eliminated in at least four ways. First, the deduction for employment plans can be eliminated. Group plans will respond by 'integrating' coverage with the accident benefit coverage. This elimination reduces the double payment described above. This approach places burdens on private insurers to predict changes in the mandatory plan. Future changes in mandatory benefits would be made more difficult because they might lead to increased short-run profits for disability insurance companies. Second, the maximum-benefits limitation could be eliminated. This would raise the cost considerably and require that automobile insurance companies determine earnings in order to charge higher premiums for those with higher earnings. Third, the first-party coverage could be eliminated altogether for those already insured under a comparable plan. This appears to be the most reasonable approach, provided that mandatory insurance coverage (without redistribution) is considered desirable. A drawback is the cost of determining if someone is covered elsewhere. Fourth, mandatory coverage could be eliminated altogether. In its stead an income-tested program could be implemented.

The accident benefits coverage, like all other private coverage, is not indexed for inflation. For those totally disabled and eligible for coverage beyond two years, the real value of the benefits will be substantially reduced. This is a serious problem which should be remedied.

PRIVATE LONG-TERM DISABILITY INSURANCE

Private long-term disability insurance is necessary if individuals are to be covered for non-work illnesses and non-work accidents in which there is no possibility of tort recovery. The CPP does not provide adequate coverage for these contingencies. Private coverage will also be desired by those not covered by workmen's compensation and those wishing greater protection than that provided by workmen's compensation. In 1977 the Canadian Association of Accident and Sickness Insurers (CAASI) reported that 2 644 245 individuals were covered by long-term disability insurance. This represents 27.1 per cent of employment in Canada (Table 5). In Ontario, 32.6 per cent of employees were covered. The growth of group disability plans has been substantial. The number of covered employees

TABLE 5

1977 Coverage for long-term disability

	Ontario	Canada
Group	1 121 207	2 310 428
Individual	104 710	333 817
Total	1 225 917	2 644 245
Percentage of employment	32.6	27.1

SOURCE: Canadian Association of Accident and Sickness Insurers; employment data from Statistics Canada, *Labour Force Survey*
NOTE: These data cover approximately 90 per cent of all insurers.

grew by 321 per cent between 1969 and 1977. Another source of data on employee benefits found that 58.8 per cent of office workers and 47.5 per cent of non-office workers were covered (Pay Research Bureau 1977). Additional long-term coverage is provided through life insurance, pension plans, and supplements to workmen's compensation, but the extent of overlap with long-term disability insurance is not known.

Group long-term disability insurance tends to be concentrated in larger, unionized, high-wage establishments. The difference between the percentage coverage reported by the Pay Research Bureau and by CAASI is that the former is based on a sample of large establishments. The growth of long-term insurance should increase as smaller establishments follow the pattern set by the larger establishments. The low level of individual coverage can be explained in part by the higher costs for these policies because of selling costs and adverse selection. One of the drawbacks to the voluntary private system is that the individual buyer must bear these higher administrative costs.

The predominance of group insurance raises some interesting questions regarding the misperceptions discussed in Chapter 3. One explanation for its predominance would be that union leaders bargain for benefits that workers are not buying as individuals because the leaders have better information. This hypothesis cannot be tested because group insurance is also considerably cheaper than individual insurance.

The biggest problem that faces private disability insurance is inflation. The private insurer cannot offer fully indexed benefits in the absence of indexed assets. This deficiency can be remedied with some form of insurance scheme for disability and retirement pension funds. As a partial remedy, consumption-stabilizing annuities (Chapter 4) would lower the risk to the annuitant without exposing insurance companies to the risk of unanticipated inflation. Without

Evaluation of existing programs 101

indexation, the private coverage will always be inadequate, and there will be increasing pressure for public coverage.

Current attempts to integrate plans pose another threat to private insurance as a widely used method for providing insurance protection. The recent changes in accident benefits and the Wyatt (1978) proposals for deducting private benefits from workmen's compensation both discourage private group insurance.

TORT COMPENSATION

Although the economic literature stresses the efficiency aspects of tort law, the participants in the legal process appear to be largely concerned with the compensation awarded to the plaintiffs. The Pearson Commission paid little attention to the efficiency aspects of torts, noting that 'tort does not have a criminal or punitive function; it is meant to compensate the injured plaintiff for actual loss or damage' (Great Britain 1978, 68). This view is inconsistent with the fact that victims receive compensation only when there is fault. This conflict between the efficiency and compensation objectives has led courts to be quick to find fault when faced with deserving plaintiffs. Consequently, this system is slowly moving towards strict liability for sellers or manufacturers of consumer products through court decisions and legislation such as the Saskatchewan Consumer Products Warranties Act.

Strict liability is equivalent to insurance provided by the sellers of products. This insurance cost will be largely borne by the consumer, not the manufacturer. Therefore the appropriate level of compensation provides benefits to the point where the marginal utilities of income are equated between the healthy and disabled states of the world, with adjustment if there is moral hazard. This amount is likely to be approximated by pecuniary loss, with no amount paid for 'pain and suffering.' The present system attempts to provide full compensation, an objective inconsistent with optimal insurance. In practice, the tort compensation is usually less than complete, particularly for serious injuries. Where a class of plaintiffs does not have a contractual relationship with the defendant and will not bear the cost of providing benefits, full compensation may be economically appropriate because it encourages an appropriate level of precautions by potential defendants.[5]

Once there is strict liability for consumer products, the elaborate tort process becomes an unnecessarily cumbersome method of awarding compensation. Legal

---

5 If the plaintiff also influences the level of safety, the optimal award may be somewhat less.

102 Disability insurance and public policy

issues still remain, such as whether an accident was caused by a defective product, but there is little advantage in using the courts to administer benefits. Similarly, if all parties are insured, such as in the automobile case, the efficiency gains from the tort system are small in relation to the inefficiency of torts as a method of administering benefits.

SICK LEAVE AND SICKNESS INSURANCE

Although a first impression might lead one to suggest that workers should insure themselves against short-term illness, three factors tend to diminish the attractiveness of this type of coverage. First, for a given individual there may be relatively little year-to-year variation in the number of days lost because of illness. If there is no variation, there is no risk, only certainty of income loss. Second, there may be moral hazard. Those insured for sickness are less likely to return to work when not feeling well. Others may even feign illness. Third, if illness is of short duration, the administrative costs of an insurance scheme may be large relative to the benefits of insurance.

It is informative to examine the types of short-term illness coverage that are in fact provided in the private sector. The most comprehensive analysis of employment provisions is carried out by the Pay Research Bureau of the Public Service Staff Relations Board. Their analysis of compensation packages covers establishments with 75 per cent of employees in an industry beginning with the largest establishments. Tables 6-8 summarise the provisions found in the survey. There are basically two types of coverage: sick leave and sickness indemnity. Sick leave includes programs in which employees are allowed a fixed number of days of illness a year. Sickness indemnity is a formal insurance plan.

There are significant differences between the two types of sickness compensation. In many ways sick leave is not really insurance. Often sick leave is accumulated from year to year and unused sick days are ultimately compensated. There is no insurance in this type of sick leave because variation in illness affects the worker's total compensation. Those who escape illness can collect the monetary equivalent of sick leave. In Table 7 only 11.5 per cent of employees in the Pay Research Bureau sample were working under this provision. However, in Ontario collective agreements (covering more than two hundred employees) 90 per cent of those with sick leave were allowed to accumulate credits (Ontario 1976). If sick leave can be claimed regardless of whether one is actually ill, those who are ill lose leisure time compared to healthy individuals. Most sick leave plans do not require a medical certificate for illness of only a few days duration. It is not surprising that sick leave provisions do not usually have a waiting period. There

TABLE 6

Incidence of insurance for short-term illness as an employment benefit, 1966

Prevalence	Employment (%)	
	Office	Non-Office
Paid sick leave	68.0	35.4
Sickness indemnity insurance	15.0	53.7
Both	16.9	10.1
No insurance	0.0	0.8
	100.0	100.0

SOURCE: Pay Research Bureau (1977, 29)

TABLE 7

Characteristics of paid sick leave provisions, 1976

	Employment (%)	
	Office	Non-office
Waiting period		
Yes	2.9	17.1
No	97.1	82.9
Leave cumulative		
Yes	33.4	57.2
No	66.6	42.8
Full pay		
Yes	61.9	64.9
No	38.1	35.1
Unused sick leave credits		
Compensated	11.5	19.2
Not compensated	23.6	38.5
No credit accumulation	64.9	42.3
Medical certificate required after		
Any absence	3.0	9.8
2-3 days	22.4	34.0
4-5 days	29.8	13.2
over 6 days	2.5	1.6
Varies	2.5	0.8
Management discretion	32.1	32.6
Never	7.7	8.0

SOURCE: Pay Research Bureau (1977 29-20)

TABLE 8

Characteristics of sickness indemnity plans for non-office workers 1976

	% of Employment
Waiting period	
3 days or less	41.2
4-7 days	53.1
10-12 days	0.7
None	4.4
No information	0.6
	100.0
Benefit Formulas	
Percentage of Earnings	
Under 66.6 %	8.3
66.6%	21.5
70-75%	1.6
100%	1.6
Varies	26.6
Fixed dollars a week	39.7
No information	0.6
	100.0
Maximum Duration	
Under 26 weeks	3.5
26 weeks	51.9
27-51 weeks	1.0
52 weeks	40.4
Varies and no information	3.2
	100.0

SOURCE: Pay Research Bureau (1977, 31)

is no need for a waiting period when the worker has no incentive to increase the frequency of his claim.

Sickness indemnity plans are regular insurance programs. In contrast to sick leave, almost all plans have a waiting period, offer less than full pay, and require a medical certificate (Table 8). These characteristics are adjustments to the moral hazard which exists for this type of insurance. In most cases the plans offer one-half year to one year's benefits, which greatly exceeds the usual coverage under sick leave. Nevertheless, the average sickness indemnity plan is less expensive than sick leave because of the greater control over claims. For the employer a formal plan has the advantage of relinquishing the responsibility for difficult administrative decisions to an insurance company (Coward 1977, 172).

Sick leave tends to predominate in office work while sickness indemnity prevails in non-office employment. The reasons for this difference are complex but reflect, in part, the lower level of flexibility of non-office work. In an office situation, work can more easily be postponed and performed after a period of absence. In contrast, the absence of a non-office worker may impose much higher costs on the employer. These costs will induce the firm to make greater effort to discourage absences by monitoring illnesses.

Although utility theory suggests that in the absence of transaction costs the benefits of insuring large losses are much greater than for small losses, virtually all employees in the Pay Research Bureau survey were covered for short-term illness, and only 47.5 per cent of non-office and 58.8 per cent of office workers were insured for long-term disability (Pay Research Bureau 1977, 35). This suggests that there is too much emphasis on 'insuring' more certain events such as short-term illness rather than more remote long-term disability.

UNEMPLOYMENT INSURANCE

The unemployment insurance (UI) program provides up to fifteen weeks of benefits for unemployment caused by illness after a two-week waiting period. A minimum of twenty weeks of contributions is required for eligibility. The benefit rate is now 60 per cent of insurable earnings. These benefits cannot be paid to someone earning a full workmen's compensation benefit. In contrast to most government programs, employers can reduce their UI contribution rates if they provide equivalent private insurance schemes. In effect, UI provides short-term sickness insurance for those not covered by employer programs. However, groups such as the self-employed are not covered by unemployment insurance.

The UI illness benefits are subject to the same criticisms as the private short-term plan. For someone eligible for long-term benefits, such as under the CPP, the illness benefits effectively reduce the waiting period to two weeks. This defeats the purpose of the CPP waiting period. The fact that UI benefits are higher than CPP benefits demonstrates the inadequacy of the latter.

Since the argument for short-term illness benefits from an insurance point of view is weak, the argument for mandatory short-term benefits is even weaker. The UI program, including regular as well as illness benefits, is not really an insurance scheme but an income-support scheme that is unrelated to income. The short-term illness benefits, like the regular UI benefits, would more effectively satisfy the most urgent needs if they were paid on an income-tested basis.

WELFARE

Those in Ontario with low incomes are eligible for income-tested programs if they are disabled or permanently unemployable. These benefits are administered along with other programs under the Family Benefits Act. The programs have a substantial disincentive to work that arises because unemployability is best demonstrated by not working. Once accepted, a beneficiary loses 75 per cent of earnings over $60 per month. When income taxes and contributions to unemployment insurance and the CPP are taken into account, the total tax-back rate climbs to over 100 per cent in some cases. A lower tax rate would encourage additional work and perhaps lead to departure from the insurance program. The lower tax rate should apply to in-kind benefits provided to the disabled as well as cash benefits. The disadvantage of a lower tax rate is that additional individuals would qualify for benefits.

Another unrealistic feature of welfare is the treatment of liquid assets. Benefits are not paid as long as liquid assets exceed $1500. This does little to encourage long-range planning of consumption. A more sensible approach would be to assume that the purchasing power represented by the liquid assets would be spread out over the lifetime or duration of disability. Annuity tables would suggest an amount that could be consumed in each year. This amount should be deducted from annual benefits, rather than the entire excess over $1500. The deduction of public and private periodic payments is reasonable if the program is designed to provide a minimum level of insurance for those without alternatives.

The welfare benefits in Ontario are not automatically indexed for inflation. In fact, a cost-of-living adjustment to CPP benefits, for example, will result in a corresponding decrease in welfare benefits. This procedure allows benefits to fall in real terms despite the increases in CPP benefits.

GROUPS NOT COVERED

The present system of disability programs covers the population to different degrees, depending on the extent or type of employment and the origins of the disability. The Canada Pension Plan covers virtually all workers, but has too strict requirements for the number of years of contributions before coverage. Workmen's compensation omits some groups such as 'domestic or menial servants.' Employers and the self-employed are not mandatorily covered. Except for CPP benefits, non-occupational accidents and long-term illnesses are not covered in the absence of private insurance, unless tort compensation or automobile accident benefits are payable.

Evaluation of existing programs 107

The largest group of uninsured individuals consists of those who do not work in the labour market or who earn minimal amounts in the labour market. The only specific benefits in Ontario for those outside the labour force are $70 a week for twelve weeks provided to a 'principal unpaid housekeeper' under the accident benefits insurance. The lack of coverage for non-workers is not necessarily irrational. First, moral hazard is probably greatest for this group because the cost of claiming benefits is very low. Workers must give up earnings in order to claim benefits. Second, optimal insurance suggests that only pecuniary losses should be compensated if the marginal utility of income is unaffected; thus the insurable loss is considerably lower for someone outside the labour force. The value of lost home production is extremely difficult to calculate. It is more logical to provide benefits based on need than to impose an insurance program on those groups for whom it is inappropriate.

7
Conclusions

INSURANCE MARKETS AND SOCIAL INSURANCE

A great deal of the discussion of disability compensation systems and safety regulation ignores the fact that there is a market for insurance and safety in which individuals' preferences for these commodities are expressed, given the cost constraints. Policies designed without consideration of this market will run into a number of difficulties. First, since the consumer's desired level of insurance or safety may already be satisfied in the market, government insurance, if it differs from the voluntary coverage, may eliminate the private coverage and reduce utility. Second, insurance levels will adjust in response to government policies. Although the public policy may reflect a more accurate assessment of risk than consumers are able to make, the subsequent response of consumers to policies such as mandatory insurance could lower their utility.

A third reason for considering the insurance market is that it provides valuable information for those designing social insurance programs. For example, a lack of market insurance for some groups or activities may indicate significant moral hazard, and a government program that ignores this problem will be extermely inefficient. Despite the equity objective the preferred public program may include differential contributions and benefits in order to encourage an efficient level of safety precautions and reduce moral hazard. The desirability of such segmentation depends on the cost of precautions, the cost of monitoring losses, the response of individuals to the availability of benefits, and the degree of risk aversion. The experience of the private market provides some guidance in evaluating these factors.

In many markets information problems can be ignored, but it should be clear from this study that imperfect information is a major factor in insurance markets and in the design of social insurance programs. The cost of acquiring information on precautions and risk levels leads to adverse selection, statistical discrimination, and insurance rates that imperfectly reflect risk. The cost of determining the size of the loss influences the benefit schedule and leads to adjustments in the extent and duration of disability in response to the insurance.

The imperfect information is present for the administrators of social insurance programs as well as for private insurance carriers. The difficulties in designing an unemployment insurance system so that premiums correspond to risk and the problem of determining who is involuntarily unemployed are perfect illustrations of the role that imperfect information plays in any social insurance scheme. The effect of generous unemployment insurance benefit levels on the measured unemployment rate is now widely accepted. A similar problem must be avoided in the design of a disability insurance system.

Although social insurance programs are often intended to redistribute income to particular groups, such as the disabled, the insurance analogy is still relevant. The expected utility of a target group can be maximized by moving income between the healthy and disabled states of the world. If the redistribution objective aims at only helping the disabled group after they are disabled, the practical problem of determining who is disabled must be faced. This is the same problem that arises in determining the extent of a loss due to disability in an insurance program, and the eligibility criteria for the redistributive program should be based on similar criteria because both programs face the same costs of acquiring information.

REFORMS OF SPECIFIC PROGRAMS

Several changes in existing policies would make a tremendous improvement in the existing system. The most important reforms are taxation of disability benefits and indexation of both public and private benefits. For reasons explained in Chapter 4 the taxation of workmen's compensation benefits is extremely important. Wyatt (1978), Saskatchewan (1976), and Manitoba (1977) have all attempted to improvise methods of taxing workmen's compensation benefits internally. This process could be done more efficiently along with the taxation of other income. The additional revenues could assist the Workmen's Compensation Board in meeting the unfunded liability created by indexation of benefits.

Individual disability benefits should also be taxed when received and deductible as contributions. This allows insurance carriers to relate the disability benefit to the total loss and puts individual policy-holders on the same footing as members of employer plans. Deductibility of contributions to individual policies might also draw attention to disability insurance for those who might not have realized that they needed it.

There is absolutely no reason why the Ontario Workmen's Compensation Board cannot index benefits for inflation, a move that would eliminate a great deal of the criticism of the present compensation system. It may also eliminate some of the need for private supplementation of workmen's compensation in the case of long-term disability. Automatic indexation would also simplify the funding of workmen's compensation because the escalation would be pre-funded. The current adjustments result in increased liabilities of present and future employers and employees for past accidents.

Private disability plans along with private pension plans have greater difficulties in providing indexed benefits, yet without indexation private benefits may provide little in the way of insurance. A partial solution would be the introduction of consumption-stabilizing annuities, described in Chapter 4. A more complete solution is Pesando's (1979) proposal, also suggested by the Pearson Commission, which calls for government inflation insurance for disability and retirement pensions. Another possibility is the creation of government-issued indexed bonds. Some solution is necessary if private insurance and pension plans are to survive in periods when the rate of inflation is uncertain and there is significant pressure for government insurance and pensions.

VOLUNTARY COVERAGE

By far the most important public policy issue related to disability compensation is whether the government should make insurance mandatory. It seems to be taken for granted that mandatory insurance is needed. In Canada this approach began with the introduction of workmen's compensation and continued with unemployment insurance and the Canada Pension Plan. There are proposals to extend mandatory workmen's compensation to non-work accidents. The elimination of fault-based compensation is being suggested for automobile accidents along with mandatory insurance coverage. Yet there is no reason why elimination of fault must be linked to mandatory insurance.

The arguments for mandatory insurance were carefully considered in Chapter 3. None of the arguments was convincing under close scrutiny. Even if there is widespread misperception of risk, mandatory insurance could make the public worse off. Adverse selection could justify mandatory insurance under some circumstances, but it is not at all certain if these conditions exist. In any event, some of the adverse selection problems are eliminated by group insurance. Externalities are a valid economic justification for mandatory insurance, but the externalities associated with disability may not be significant. These externalities may suggest that an income-tested program is desirable, rather than mandatory insurance for everyone. Finally, the argument that mandatory insurance is necessary because welfare programs discourage private insurance implies that the poor should pay for their own welfare.

GUARANTEED INCOME

If mandatory insurance as a general policy is rejected, there is still room for a program that would provide benefits based on need for those who could not purchase private insurance, did not perceive the risks they faced, or did not have the opportunity to 'buy' low-cost group insurance. Such a program would operate like a negative income tax, with a less than 100 per cent tax on earnings to preserve work incentives and a 100 per cent tax on private insurance benefits (as suggested in Appendix B) and workmen's compensation. This program would be limited to those demonstrating disability, whether from illness or accident. It would differ from mandatory insurance only in that it would be meant to provide basic consumption goods, not to replace a large fraction of lost income. It might have somewhat higher benefits than under current welfare programs, but it would differ from welfare only in its image as an insurance benefit.

A guaranteed income for the disabled would not be financed out of contributions and would therefore result in an increase in expected income for low-income individuals. It could replace no-fault accident benefits, unemployment insurance illness benefits, and Canada Pension Plan disability benefits, each of which provide only minimal levels of support. It would also replace existing income-tested programs such as GAINS-D. Furthermore, the existence of the guaranteed income program would take the pressure off the courts to find ways of compensating victims of accidents. The guaranteed income benefits should be deducted from damages paid to plaintiffs and instead paid to the guaranteed income system.

The guaranteed income, coupled with elimination of CPP benefits, no-fault accident benefits, and unemployment insurance illness benefits, would have some advantages for the higher-income individual who may bear the cost of the program. The current patchwork of programs insures some individuals twice for the same loss of income or provides insurance coverage beyond the level that would be chosen voluntarily. For example, the combination of tax-free workmen's compensation benefits and CPP benefits may exceed the lost net income. Reductions in the contributions and benefits can make the overinsured person better off. Consequently, some redistribution could simultaneously be accomplished without making the overinsured person worse off. The same argument applies to other cost savings. Those paying taxes to support the guaranteed

112 Disability insurance and public policy

income would no longer have to bear the high administrative costs associated with multiple programs and would not have to compensate insurance companies that provide supplemental benefits for bearing the risk of changes in public benefit levels. There would be some loss of economic efficiency because low-income individuals would no longer be making contributions in relation to their employment (CPP or UI) or ownership of an automobile (accident benefits). These losses might be offset if private insurance carriers tailor their rates more closely to risk-exposure than public programs do. Private coverage will probably expand as CPP, UI, and accident benefits are dropped.

A guaranteed-income system for the disabled would solve some of the problems presented by the lack of coverage for those not working in the labour market. It is extremely difficult to design an insurance program for this group. The guaranteed income concept accepts the moral hazard as a necessary side-effect only in the case of low-income families.

A serious drawback to a guaranteed income aimed solely at the disabled is that the costs of determining disability are high. However, these costs may not be higher than the costs in the current disability benefit programs that would be eliminated. A further problem with a generous disability program is that individuals with no other source of income supplementation will have an incentive to feign disability, reducing their work significantly in order to demonstrate it. A universal guaranteed income would avoid these problems but would transfer benefits to a large segment of the population.

NO-FAULT

The efficiency that the tort system attempts to achieve is mitigated by the existence of insurance for most potential plaintiffs and defendants. Furthermore, the courts have not been particularly good institutions for assessing losses. Many advocates of no-fault systems have based their recommendations on a preference for periodic payments rather than lump-sum payments. It was demonstrated in Chapter 4 that lump-sum payments may be preferable, but in any event the no-fault issue need not be tied to the choice between forms of payment. Rather, it should be made on efficiency grounds.

The role of liability in influencing behaviour in automobiles is limited by the widespread existence of insurance coverage. Furthermore, there are alternatives to liability as a means of influencing behaviour, such as traffic fines and licensing standards. Removal of the right to sue under tort law following an automobile accident is usually accompanied by mandatory insurance for automobile drivers, their passengers, and pedestrians. The owner of the automobile pays for this insurance. For example, the Quebec Automobile Insurance Act provides mandatory insurance that replaces 90 per cent of net income, indexed for inflation. If

Conclusions 113

mandatory insurance is not considered necessary and a guaranteed income plan provides benefits to those with few other sources of income, there is no reason to have mandatory insurance as part of the no-fault legislation. An exception would be insurance to cover non-drivers and non-residents who may not anticipate the uniqueness of a no-fault jurisdiction and who would not be eligible for a guaranteed income.

The only reason for requiring that a driver insure himself, his passengers, and pedestrians against injury is to assign the cost of driving to the driver. The intention is to induce him to make an efficient decision on whether to own a car and on the appropriate precautions to take. The scope for these incentives is small, because of the difficulty of determining which drivers pose the greatest risks. Similarly, strict liability for consumer products may not lead to more efficiency than a system without any liability.

Complete elimination of liability may not be politically feasible at the present time, but it will become a more obvious step if some of the other recommendations described above are implemented. Taxation of workmen's compensation, deductibility of contributions for individual disability insurance, and indexation of private benefits will allow the private disability insurance industry to offer a better product, which in turn will be demanded by increasing numbers of individuals. Wider private insurance coverage and a viable guaranteed income for those with health impairments and low income will reduce the need for tort law as a method of compensation and will expose tort law to greater scrutiny as a mechanism for inducing efficient behaviour. Tort law may not survive this increased scrutiny.

APPENDIX A

Adverse selection and mandatory insurance

The adverse selection problem can best be illustrated with an insurance market with only two types of customers, high-risk and low-risk. The two types have identical preference functions but different levels of risk. The following analysis is derived from Wilson (1977).

It is assumed that the insurance companies cannot invest in information that would allow them to distinguish high-risk individuals, but each individual knows the risk he faces. For each individual there is a set of indifference curves between the insurance premium and the indemnity (gross of the premium). At any given premium and indemnity the indifference curves for the high-risk person are steeper. In Figure A.1 the indifference curves of the high- and low-risk individuals are indicated with a superscript H or L. Firms are assumed to offer contracts which are a combination of a premium and an indemnity, and it is assumed for the moment that only one contract can be purchased per customer. The fair odds lines are indicated by OP_L and OP_H. If insurers could indentify them, the high-risk customers would be offered policy S^2 and the low-risk customers would be offered S^3.[1] The dashed line represents optimal insurance coverage; in other words, marginal utilities of income are equated in both states of the world for the individual.

In the absence of an ability to distinguish between customers the nature of the market outcome depends on the firm's perception of its own actions on the market. Wilson (1977) analysed the importance of alternative assumptions. It is assumed here that there will be an equilibrium when each contract earns non-negative profits. Each firm assumes that other firms will not react to the introduction of a new policy. In Figure A.1, S^3 could not be offered because it would earn negative profits if purchased by a high-risk individual. Instead S^1 and S^2

---

1 Note that the indemnity is the same for both high- and low-risk individuals, assuming $U'' = V''$, because it is gross of the premium paid.

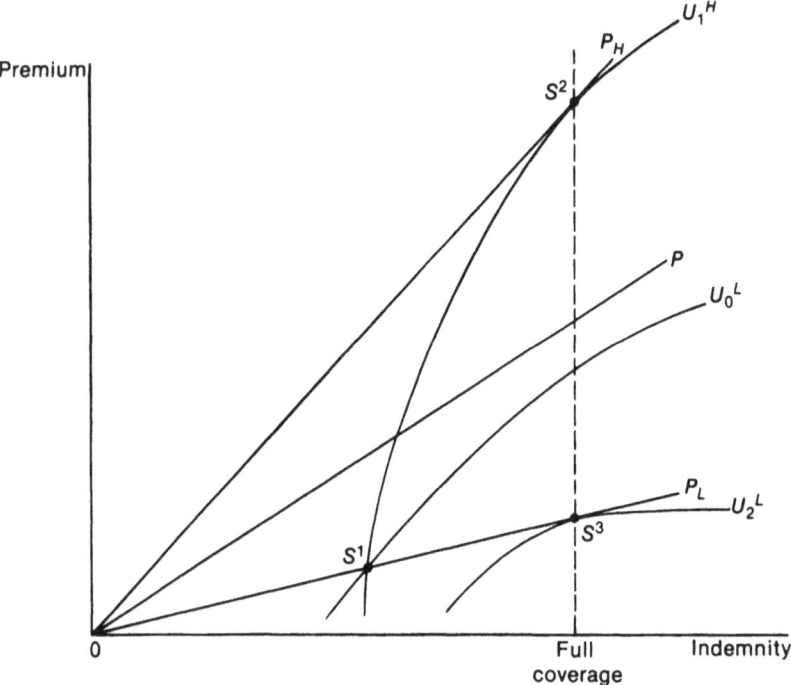

Figure A.1: Adverse selection: pooling equilibrium

will be offered. S^1 is the maximum coverage that can be offered to low-risk customers without attracting high-risk customers, because the latter are indifferent between S^1 and S^2. S^1 will be chosen by the low-risk person and S^2 by the high-risk person. The low-risk person is suboptimally insured because of the presence of high-risk individuals. In this case there is an equilibrium in the market (called a 'separating equilibrium' by Rothschild and Stiglitz, 1976) because there is no alternative policy that would earn non-negative profits.

OP is the fair odds line when two types of individuals are pooled. As long as OP lies above the indifference curve U_0L that passes through S^1, low-risk individuals cannot be attracted to a pooled policy that is also purchased by those with higher risks. If OP falls below U_0L, there will exist alternative pooled policies which appear to earn non-negative profits (S^0 in Figure A.2), but there will not be an equilibrium in the industry. Note that an increase in the proportion of low risk individuals will lower OP and increase the probability that the combination S^1 and S^2 is not an equilibrium.

Adverse selection and mandatory insurance   117

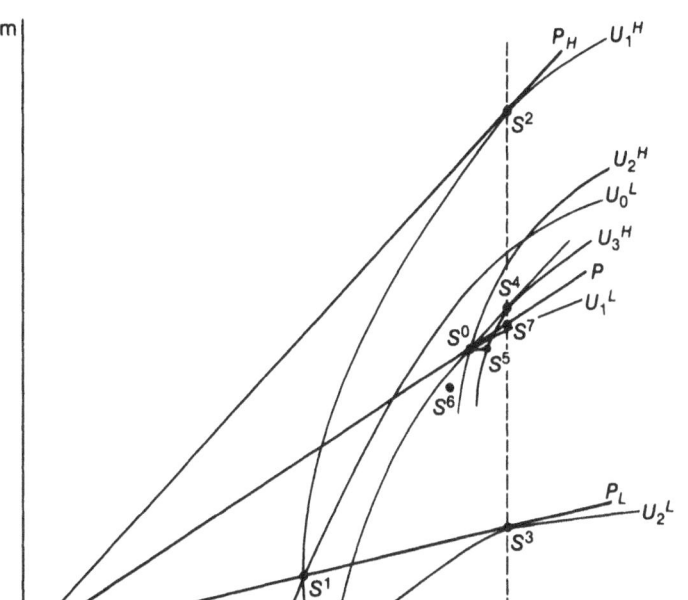

Figure A.2: Adverse selection: separating equilibrium

Under the definition of equilibrium described above there is either an equilibrium in which separate policies are purchased by high- and low-risk individuals or there is no equilibrium at all (Figure A.2). The lack of equilibrium occurs because new policies that appear to be profitable (such as S^6 in Figure A.2) make existing policies (S^0) unprofitable because low-risk people are attracted to the new policies. Wilson (1977) suggests that firms will learn through experience to anticipate the effect of new policies on old policies. Under his alternative assumptions S^0 will be an equilibrium (a pooling equilibrium).

The equilibrium policy S^0 provides suboptimal insurance for both high- and low-risk individuals. It is interesting to speculate whether the market would provide supplemental coverage if more than one policy can be purchased. If firms do not know what other policies are being purchased but can limit total purchases to the value of the loss, high-risk individuals will be offered supplemental coverage that will move them to S^4. They will be fully insured, but supplemental coverage cannot be offered to the low-risk individuals because it would be purchased by the high-risk individuals. If insurance companies know which other policies are purchased by the customer, they might make a purchase of S^0 conditional on the non-purchase of extra coverage in order to attract more favourable risks. This would destroy the market for the supplemental coverage.

The sub-optimality of coverage suggests that the government could make the insurance market more efficient. One possibility is to require full coverage for everyone (S^7). Given the price of this coverage, the low-risk individuals will prefer less coverage (S^0). The movement from S^0 to S^7 makes the high-risk individuals better off at the expense of the low-risk individuals. This move may be a desirable redistribution of income because the high-risk individuals have lower expected incomes. However, a stronger case can be made for a move away from S^0 that will make both groups better off.

Wilson suggests two possible government strategies. The first is to require all insurance companies to issue S^0 policies (unconditional on the purchase of supplemental coverage). The private market would then provide supplemental coverage that would move high-risk individuals to S^4 and low-risk persons to S^5. High-risk individuals would be fully insured and would be better off than at S^2 because of the implicit subsidy by low-risk persons on the mandatory insurance. Full coverage cannot be provided to the low-risk individuals without attracting those with high risk.

The second alternative is for the government to offer S^4 and S^5 as alternative policies. S^5 will be chosen by high-risk individuals and S^4 by low-risk individuals. This combination breaks even in the aggregate but violates the assumption that each policy earn non-negative profits. The policy sold to low-risk individuals earns a profit that subsidizes the high-risk individuals. Nevertheless, the low-risk individuals prefer S^5 to the market outcome at S^0 (which is a Wilson equilibrium point). Another interpretation of this result is that a firm may negotiate with insurance companies for a group policy for its employees with optional supplementary coverage. The employees would prefer this type of group coverage to the individual coverage available in the market.[2]

The policies described above may not be applicable if a separating equilibrium exists, as in Figure A.1. Figure A.3 illustrates a situation in which a separating equilibrium can be improved upon by government-imposed mandatory coverage up to S^6 or by having the government offer two policies S^4 and S^5 (Wilson 1977, 48).

If the government is constrained to intervene in the insurance markets only if a Pareto-optimal change can be made, it must know a great deal about prefer-

---

2 It is assumed that the distribution of high- and low-risk employees in the firm remains unchanged after the group policy goes into effect.

Adverse selection and mandatory insurance 119

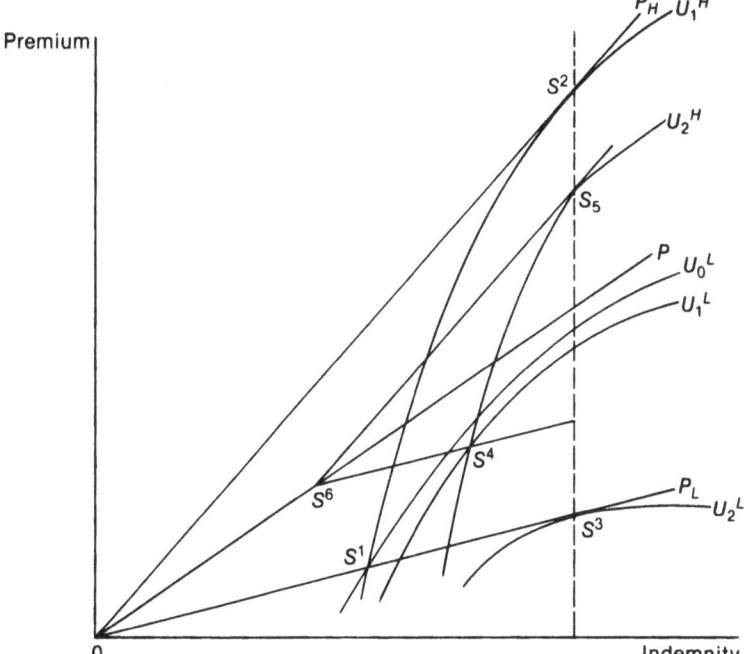

Figure A.3: Adverse selection: separating equilibrium with mandatory insurance

ences of individuals and the distribution of risks. If it makes a mistake in choosing the mandatory insurance level it could make the low-risk group worse off. An increase in mandatory coverage up to S^6 in Figure A.3 or S^0 in Figure A.2 will benefit both groups, but an increase beyond S^6 or S^0 will benefit high-risk individuals at the expense of low-risk individuals (compared to S^6 or S^0). In other words, any move towards mandatory coverage will benefit those with higher risks and may or may not benefit those with lower risks.

The relative number of high- and low-risk individuals is an important piece of information for policy determination. Other things equal, the greater the number of low-risk individuals the greater the chances of a pooled equilibrium and the greater the probability that mandatory coverage will make both groups better off. Conversely, the greater the relative number of high-risk individuals the greater the chances of a separating equilibrium and the smaller the probability that mandatory coverage will make the low-risk group better off. Mandatory coverage is more likely to be a move towards Pareto optimality if there are relatively few high-risk individuals.[3] The potential gains become small, however, because S^0 in Figure A.2 approaches the full insurance point as the number of high-risk individuals goes to zero. The greater the difference in risk between the two individuals, the more likely there will be a separating equilibrium and the less likely mandatory insurance will make the low-risk group better off. This is obvious in the case in which the low-risk group faces no risk at all. If there are many risk groups, the chances of improving every group's position as a result of mandatory insurance is smaller than with fewer risk types.

---

[3] Even if the social welfare function suggests redistribution towards the high-risk group, the social welfare gains for a given transfer are also reduced as the low-risk group becomes smaller.

APPENDIX B

Income-tested government programs and mandatory insurance

IMPACT OF WELFARE PROGRAMS

The decision to purchase disability insurance will be affected by government programs that provide benefits to those with low income. In order to exclude labour supply considerations, it is assumed that the government program is categorical and only available to those with a disability. It is also assumed that the administrators of both the government program and the private insurance program can costlessly ascertain whether an applicant is disabled or healthy.

The welfare program provides income in the event of disability, but the benefits paid will be negatively related to private insurance benefits m because the welfare program is designed to assist those with little alternative income. The welfare program is assumed to operate like a negative income tax for the disabled. Specifically, the benefits will equal $G - t\,m(g)$, as long as $m(g) < G/t$, where G is the guaranteed level of benefits for those with no other income and t is the implicit tax on private insurance benefits. If private insurance income exceeds G/t, called the break-even point, welfare benefits equal zero.

Given the existence of the welfare program, the individual will purchase insurance so as to maximize expected utility:

$$aU(w - g) + (1 - a)V(m(g) + G - t m(g)). \tag{B.1}$$

Expected utility is maximized if

$$U' = V'(1 - t). \tag{B.2}$$

Clearly U' will be less than V', implying that insurance coverage is less than complete. The welfare program, with its implicit tax on private benefits, will

122 Appendix B

lower the total (public and private) insurance coverage relative to the optimal coverage. As long as the benefits did not exceed the desired level, the total insurance coverage would be optimal if the welfare benefit were a lump sum. It is the income-tested nature of welfare, not the existence of an alternative to private insurance, that distorts the decision to purchase insurance.

For simplicity, it is useful to consider the case in which $U(x) = V(x) + a$ constant, for all x, that is, the disability does not affect the marginal utility of income. Let I_1 equal income in the disabled state of the world. If we start from the market equilibrium position where $t = 0$ and $G = 0$ and assume that the second-order conditions hold, it can easily be shown that

$$\partial g/\partial w = 1 - a, \tag{B.3}$$

$$\partial g/\partial G = -(1 - a), \tag{B.4}$$

$$\partial g/\partial t = (1 - a)(m + U'/U'') \leq 0, \tag{B.5}$$

$$\partial I_1/\partial w = a, \tag{B.6}$$

$$\partial I_1/\partial G = 1 - a, \tag{B.7}$$

$$\partial I_1/\partial t = -(1 - a)m + aU'/U''. \tag{B.8}$$

Holding utility constant by compensating for the tax with a change in G, we get substitution effects

$$(\partial g/\partial t)_{\bar{U}} = (1 - a)(U'/U'') < 0, \tag{B.9}$$

$$(\partial I_1/\partial t)_{\bar{U}} = a(U'/U'') < 0. \tag{B.10}$$

Therefore

$$\partial g/\partial t = (\partial g/\partial W)m + (\partial g/\partial t)_{\bar{U}}, \tag{B.11}$$

and

$$\partial I_1/\partial t = -(\partial I_1/\partial G)m + (\partial I_1/\partial t)_{\bar{U}}, \tag{B.12}$$

Income-tested government programs and mandatory insurance 123

It is apparent from equations (B.11) and (B.12) that a tax change imposes both income and substitution effects. The tax lowers income in the disabled state, inducing an increase in private insurance but a decrease in consumption in both states of the world. The substitution effect induces a decrease in private insurance and disability income. The sign of the response of private insurance to a tax on private insurance benefits is ambiguous, but total disability income unambiguously falls in response to the tax.

If we combine the guarantee with the tax change, the total response to the introduction of the welfare program for someone with private benefits initially below the break-even point $((G - mt) > 0)$ is

$$dg = -(1 - a)dG + (1 - a)(m + (U'/U''))dt \qquad (B.13)$$

$$= (1 - a)(U'/U'')t - (1 - a)(G - mt) < 0$$

$$dI_1 = (1 - a)dG + [-(1 - a)m + a(U'/U'')]dt \qquad (B.14)$$

$$= a(U'/U'')t + (1 - a)(G - mt) \lessgtr 0.$$

Private insurance falls as a result of the program, but total net benefits may rise or fall. The substitution effect decreases total benefits, but the income effect increases total benefits. In practice the income effect is small because the probability of collecting the benefits $(1 - a)$ is low. Therefore, expected income increases only a small amount in response to welfare. The substitution effect is likely to be large unless there is extreme risk-aversion, and total insurance coverage is likely to fall.

GRAPHICAL ANALYSIS OF THE INSURANCE DECISION

Since the impact of welfare on the insurance decision will depend on the optimal level of insurance as well as the tax rate and the level of benefits, a graphical analysis is useful. Figure B.1 illustrates the constraint and indifference curves for someone allocating income between the healthy and disabled states of the world. The wage, gross of insurance premiums, is w_0, and the constraint in the absence of public insurance is FJ with a slope equal to $-(1 - a)/a$. Insurance purchases are optimal where $U' = V'$, at point A on the 45° line. Income will equal aw_0 whether or not disability occurs.

Consider the effect of a lump-sum benefit equal to G on the insurance decision. The benefit shifts the constraint to the right by the amount G. The utility-

124 Appendix B

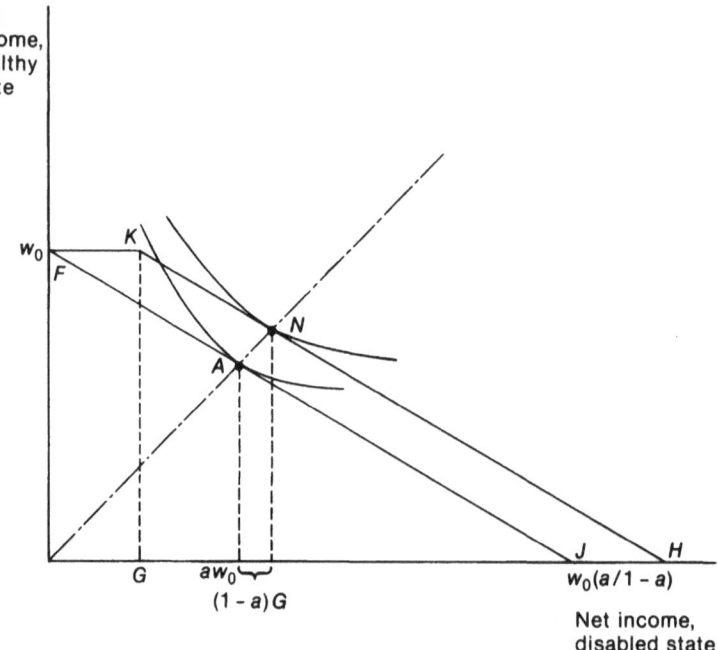

Figure B.1: The insurance decision in the presence of a lump-sum disability benefit

maximizing individual chooses point N on constraint KNH. Total public and private insurance increases by $(1 - a)G$ as a result of the increase in expected income equal to $(1 - a)G$. This income effect is small because $1 - a$ is usually a very small probability. Private insurance falls from aw_0 to $(aw_0 + (1 - a)G) - G$, which equals $a(w_0 - G)$. If w_0 equals G, private insurance falls to zero.

Usually welfare programs include a tax on other income. Consider a welfare program that provides an amount G with a tax on private insurance benefits equal to t. These parameters imply that anyone with income below G/t will receive some welfare benefits. The amount is called the break-even point. In Figure B.2 the parameters G and t are such that the individual is initially at the break-even point. For the moment it is assumed that someone else pays the taxes that finance the welfare program. The new constraint is $KNAJ$, with the slope of KNA equal to $-(1 - a)/a(1 - t)$. Insurance coverage falls because the tax on disability income induces a substitution of income in the healthy state for income in the disabled state. Every dollar of reduced private benefits is offset by t dollars of public benefits.

Income-tested government programs and mandatory insurance 125

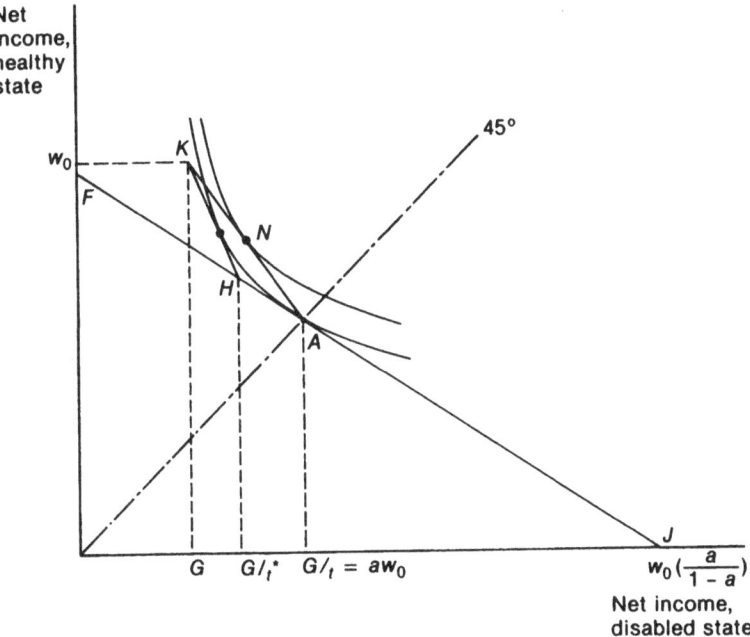

Figure B.2: The insurance decision in the presence of an income-tested welfare program

Some individuals will have optimal insurance which exceeds the break-even point ($G \div t$). Nevertheless, they may choose to reduce their private (and total) benefits in order to take advantage of the public benefits. If private coverage is reduced, net income in the healthy state increases because premiums are reduced. The desirability of reducing insurance coverage will depend on the substitutability of income in the healthy state for income in the disabled state, which in turn depends upon the extent of diminishing marginal utility of income. It follows from Rea (1974) that those with pre-welfare coverage up to $G/t - \frac{1}{2}(\partial g/\partial t)\bar{U}[a/(1-a)]t$ will choose to reduce their private insurance coverage[1] In Figure B.2 the individual who is initially at point A would choose to reduce his private coverage with a break-even level as low as G/t^*.

A third possibility is that the individual chooses to purchase no private insurance as a result of the introduction of a public program. In Figure B.2 this would

---

[1] This formula is an approximation resulting from a Taylor expansion of the utility function. The degree of error rises with the size of the tax rate.

126 Appendix B

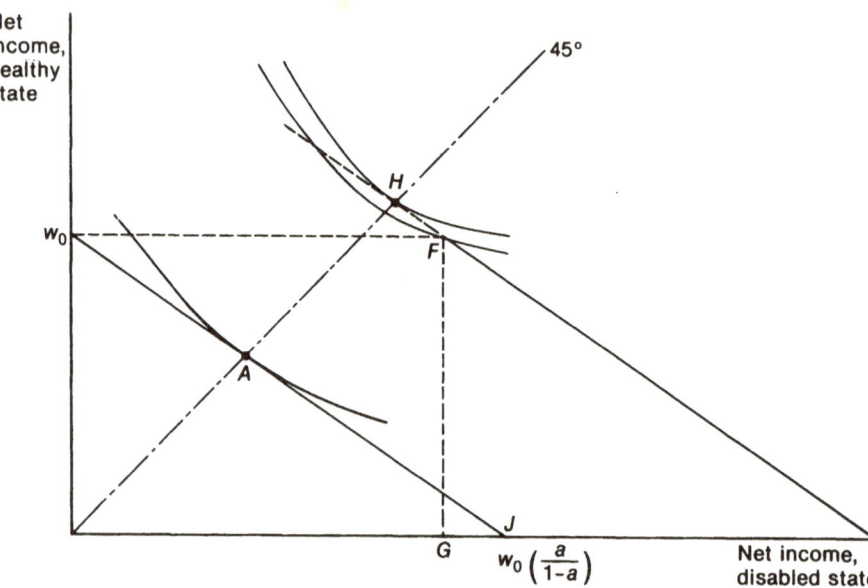

Figure B.3: The insurance decision when welfare exceeds desired insurance levels

have occurred if point K were on a higher indifference curve than point A. We shall see later that for a reasonable utility function there will be a large number of welfare recipients in this position, a conclusion that has important implications for the choice of a tax-back rate.

The final case arises when the level of public benefits exceeds the desired insurance level. In Figure B.3 the welfare program moves the person to point F. At this point the slope of his indifference curve must be flatter than $-(1 - a)/a$ because the indifference curves have this slope on the 45° line (Ehrlich and Becker 1972). Given the probability of disability, the individual would like to reduce his insurance coverage below G, but contracts that would require the individual to pay part of his welfare in the event of disability would not be legally enforceable. This individual reduces his private insurance coverage to zero, but he is overinsured when provided with welfare benefits equal to G. Notice that the tax on private benefits is irrelevant for this individual.

This situation, where disability benefits exceed wages, is often cited as a case in which there is an incentive to feign disability, a possibility not included in the model presented here because disability is assumed to be easily observed. However there is also an incentive to feign disability when earnings exceed benefits if the additional leisure is valued more highly than the loss of income. The inefficiency resulting from over-insurance derives not only from the excessive moral hazard, but also from an inappropriate allocation of the income between the healthy and disabled states of the world. In Figure B.3 the individual would be made better off by moving from F to H. The difference in utility is a deadweight loss caused by overinsurance. It is identical to the loss associated with any in-kind benefit that exceeds the quantity that the beneficiary would choose to consume.

The above analysis neglects the tax that is used to finance the benefits. Changes in program parameters will cause total benefits to change and will alter the expected income of those covered. The disincentives described above are altered slightly by the inclusion of financing costs because of income effects. Those who receive actuarially unfair benefits will suffer a loss of expected income which lowers the insurance purchased. Those who receive generous benefits relative to the taxes paid to finance the program will tend to purchase more insurance than those who pay lower taxes. If the program is actuarially fair, anyone who is purchasing both public and private insurance will suffer a deadweight loss as a result of the tax on private insurance benefits. This is shown in Figure B.4 for a representative individual. The original position is point A. The introduction of an income-tested public program will induce a reduction in private coverage and a movement to point K. Since expected net benefits are positive at this point, a tax must be levied to finance the program. A lump-sum tax on healthy-state earnings R must be found such that the individual is in equilibrium with respect to his purchases of insurance (equation B.2),

$$U'(w_0 - R - m(1-a)/a) = V'(G + (1-t)m)(1-t), \qquad (B.15)$$

and the government program breaks even:

$$R(a/(1-a)) = G - tm. \qquad (B.16)$$

These conditions are satisfied at point J in Figure B.4. The individual is on a lower indifference curve than he was at point A. The introduction of the public program makes him worse off and imposes a deadweight loss.

AN EXAMPLE

The impact of the welfare program on the insurance decision will depend on the initial optimal level of insurance relative to the welfare levels and the tax-back

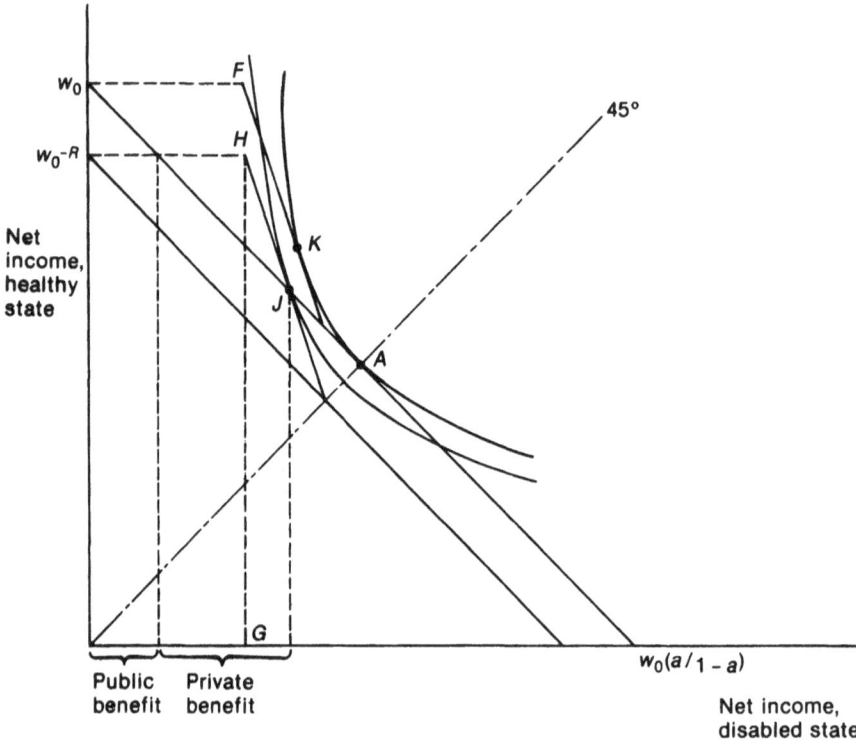

Figure B.4: The deadweight loss resulting from a tax on insurance benefits

rate. The optimal level of insurance depends on the probability of each state occurring and the level of earnings. A logarithmic utility function, which displays decreasing absolute risk-aversion and constant relative risk-aversion, can be used to illustrate the relationship between the amount of insurance and the tax rate. Assume that $U(x) = ln(x) = V(x) +$ a constant, for all x. An internal solution occurs where equation B.2 holds:

$$1/(w-g) = (1-t)/[G + g(a/(1-a))(1-t)]. \qquad (B.17)$$

Table B.1 illustrates the inter-relationship between a welfare program with a guarantee equal to $5000 and a probability of disability equal to 0.01. Column 1 indicates that someone with earnings equal to $10 000 will reduce his private insurance coverage (net of premium) from $9900 to $2475 when faced with a

TABLE B.1
Logarithmic utility function, guarantee $5000, disability probability 0.01

Tax rate (t) on private benefits (1)	Insurance purchased if $w = \$10\,000$ (1)	Break even income (2)	Gross w above which buy insurance (3)	Gross w below which choose welfare (4)	Original insurance for w in (4) (5)	Insurance after welfare for w in (4) (6)	Total public & private benefits after welfare for w in (4) (7)
0	$4 950	∞	$5 000	∞	∞	∞	∞
0.10	4 400	$50 000	5 556	$53 219	$52 687	$47 187	$47 468
0.25	3 300	20 000	6 667	23 371	23 137	16 537	17 403
0.333	2 475	15 000	7 500	18 650	18 464	11 039	12 359
0.40	1 650	12 500	8 333	16 435	16 271	8 021	9 813
0.50	0	10 000	10 000	14 521	14 376	4 476	7 238
0.60	0	8 333	12 500	13 717	13 580	1 205	5 482
0.634	0	7 886	13 660	13 660	13 523	0	5 000
0.75	0	6 667	13 660	13 660	13 523	0	5 000
1.00	0	5 000	13 660	13 660	13 523	0	5 000

Note: Columns are derived as follows:

(1) $99(100 - 50/(1-t))$
(2) $5000/t$
(3) $5000/(1-t)$
(4) $(5000/99)\,[1/(1-t)^{99}(1-t)]$ for t below 0.634
(5) $0.99 \times \text{col } 4$
(6) $0.99\,[(\text{col } 4) - 5000/(1-t)]$
(7) $5000 + (1-t)\,(\text{col } 4)$

130 Appendix B

$5000 guarantee and a 33 per cent tax in the event of disability.[2] Total coverage equals $5000 plus two-thirds of $2475, or $6650.

The third column of Table B.1 indicates the earnings level above which private insurance is purchased. This is derived by finding the value of w in equation (41) for which g equals zero, ($w = 5000/(1 - t)$). In conjunction with column 3 it is clear that for moderate values of t, such as 0.5, few individuals will supplement welfare with private insurance. Also, the reduction in private coverage is large for those who do choose supplementary coverage. For example, if $t = 0.5$, everyone with earnings below $10 000 will choose to drop private coverage. Someone with earnings equal to $14 521 would reduce his insurance coverage from $14 316 to $4476 and his total coverage from $14 376 to $7238.

Column 4 indicates the highest pre-disability earnings level of welfare recipients. This exceeds the break-even income as demonstrated in Figure B.2. When the tax rate rises above 0.634 there are no individuals who simultaneously choose welfare and supplementary private insurance.[3] At this tax rate all of those with income below $13 660 choose welfare and buy no private insurance. Those with higher incomes do not choose to qualify for welfare. Therefore any higher tax rate beyond 0.634 has no additional effect on private insurance.

The logarithmic utility function provides relatively high elasticities of substitution between income in the healthy state and income in the disabled state, as indicated by the very large effect of the tax-back rate on private insurance. This response is much greater than the observed substitution between income and leisure as a result of a negative income tax (see for example Keeley et al. 1978). For example, labour supply estimates do not suggest that a tax-back rate of 0.64 would eliminate all work by recipients. Empirical research on decisions under uncertainty could determine whether the logarithmic utility function provides an unrealistically low level of risk-avoidance.

CHOICE OF A TAX-BACK RATE

The analysis of the effect of welfare programs on private insurance raises two issues: the first is the appropriate tax on private benefits, and the second is the

---

2 This is derived by solving equation (B.17) for g, ($g = 100 - [50/(1 - t)]$). The level of insurance is $99g$.
3 This rate is determined by finding the point at which the person is indifferent between private coverage with full insurance and public coverage alone: $0.01 \ln(5000) + 0.99 \ln(w) = \ln(0.99w)$ and the optimal amount of private insurance is zero: $w = 5000/(1 - t)$.

Income-tested government programs and mandatory insurance 131

desirability of mandatory insurance in a world with pre-existing welfare programs. Welfare or disability programs include income tests in order to provide benefits to those with no alternative source of income. The tax-back rate serves to sort the disabled on the basis of income, but it produces the deadweight losses described above. As a compromise between equity and efficiency objectives, tax-back rates near 50 per cent are usually proposed for negative income taxes. In the insurance context this choice may be inappropriate if the high degree of substitution shown for the logarithmic utility function is typical.

If we introduce the program described in Table B.1 and start with a tax-back rate of 0.634, an increase in the tax rate would have no effect because no one would choose private insurance coverage. A decrease in the tax-back rate below 0.634 would induce purchases of private insurance by some of those below $13 660 in earnings, but it would lower the insurance coverage of those above this level. For instance, a reduction in the tax rate from 0.634 to 0.4 would induce someone with $10 000 in earnings to purchase only $1650 in private insurance, but it would substantially reduce the insurance coverage of all of those earning between $13 660 and $16 435. Of course one must know the number of individuals at various income levels to be sure of the exact numbers, but it appears that over some range a reduction in the tax rate below 0.634 will add to total welfare benefits, transfer benefits to high-income groups outside the target low-income population, and reduce total as well as private insurance coverage.

What are the choices open to the designer of the program? Table B.1. suggests that the disincentives to purchase private insurance are substantial and that even a small tax-back rate would have a large disincentive effect without significantly targeting the disability benefits on low-income persons. The decision concerning the tax-back rate on private insurance benefits[4] may involve only two choices, a zero tax-back rate or a 100 per cent tax-back rate. The latter targets the benefits on low-income persons but reduces private insurance to zero for the low-income population. A zero tax-back rate on private benefits will lead to a reduction in insurance by the amount of the public insurance, but there are no deadweight losses associated with this substitution. Such a program, in effect a demogrant

---

4 If there is a partial disability that cannot be accurately measured by welfare administrators, the welfare program may include a tax on earnings that is designed to vary the benefit according to the degree of disability and the degree of redistribution desired. For a given cost, this tax will be a compromise between work incentives produced by low tax rates and the greater insurance protection and redistribution offered by a higher tax rate, coupled with a higher level of benefits. The resulting tax rate will not necessarily be the same as the tax rate applied to private insurance benefits.

for the disabled, would have a high budget cost, requiring additional revenue-raising taxes which will also produce deadweight losses.

MANDATORY INSURANCE

Recognizing that income-tested programs would induce a reduction in private insurance coverage, (Musgrave 1968, 27-8) argued that mandatory insurance was required. As an example, consider the program in Table B.1 with a 100 per cent tax on private insurance ($t = 1.0$). Individuals with earnings of $13 660 or less will not purchase private insurance, because of the existence of the welfare program. Mandatory insurance would force this group to purchase at least $5000 in insurance in order to offset the disincentives caused by the income-tested welfare program. Essentially the low-income group would be forced to pay for their own welfare. This would run counter to the humanitarian objective (Musgrave's terminology). These disincentive effects of welfare programs are a price that must be paid to achieve redistribution. The argument that mandatory insurance is required to offset these disincentives implies that there should be no redistribution because the price of redistribution is positive.

One can conclude that mandatory insurance is inconsistent with the redistribution objective in a world of rational consumers, but what if there are high-income individuals who irrationally fail to insure themselves? This group is subsidized by more prudent individuals unless insurance is mandatory. It is debatable whether this consideration outweighs the inequitable effects of imposing mandatory insurance on low-income individuals. Welfare can subsidize irrationality of all types, such as poor decisions on investment in both human and non-human capital. The costs of preventing such decisions may be very high, particularly if regulators or law-makers have less information concerning each case than the individual involved.

Income-tested welfare programs will thus induce a substitution of public for private disability insurance coverage. This substitution induces deadweight losses whenever the tax on private benefits exceeds zero. There are additional deadweight losses whenever there is overinsurance. If the logarithmic utility function is a reasonable portrayal of the extent of risk-aversion, there is a high degree of substitution as a result of the tax-back rate, suggesting that a 100 per cent tax-back rate may be the best compromise between efficiency and equity objectives. Although welfare programs may induce substantial disincentives to purchase private insurance, it does not follow that mandatory disability insurance is desirable. Mandatory insurance would cancel out the intended redistributive effects of the welfare program.[5]

---

5 Large-scale irrationality on the part of high-income individuals could alter this conclusion, but asset tests included in welfare programs may alleviate this problem.

Bibliography

Akerlof, G.A. (1978) 'The economics of "tagging" as applied to the optimal income tax, welfare programs, and manpower planning.' *American Economic Review* 68, 8-19

Arrow, K.J. (1963) 'Uncertainty and the welfare economics of medical care.' *American Economic Review* 52, 941-73

Australia (1974) Report of the National Committee of Inquiry *Compensation and Rehabilitation in Australia*

Bailey, M.J. (1978) 'Safety decisions and insurance.' *American Economic Review* 68 295-300

Bartel, A. and P. Taubman (1979) "Health and labor market success: the role of various diseases.' *Review of Economics and Statistics* 61, 1-9

Becker, G.S. (1965) 'A theory of the allocation of time.' *Economic Journal* 75, 493-517

Berkowitz, M., V. Englander, J. Rubin, and J.D. Worrall (1975) *An Evaluation of Policy-Related Rehabilitation Research* (New York: Praeger)

Berkowitz, M., W.G. Johnson, and E.H. Murphy (1976) *Public Policy toward Disability* (New York: Praeger)

Berkowitz, M. and J.F. Burton (1970) 'The income-maintenance objective in workmen's compensation' *Industrial and Labor Relations Review* 24, 14-31

Berkowitz, M. and W.G. Johnson (1970) 'Towards an economics of disability: the magnitude and structure of transfer and medical costs.' *Journal of Human Resources* 5, 271-97

– (1974) 'Health and labor force participation.' *Journal of Human Resources* 9, 115-28

Brinker, P.A. and E.W. Murdock (1973) 'Children of the severely injured.' *Journal of Human Resources* 8, 242-9

British Columbia (1968) Royal Commission on Automobile Insurance in British Columbia *Report*

Brittain, J.A. (1972) *The Payroll Tax for Social Security* (Washington DC: The Brookings Institution)

Broussalian, V.L. (1975) 'Risk measurement and safety standards in consumer products.' In N.E. Terleckyj, ed., *Household Production and Consumption* (New York: National Bureau of Economic Research)

Brown, J.C. (1977) *A Hit-And-Miss Affair* (Ottawa: Canadian Council on Social Development)

Brown, J.P. (1973) 'Towards an economic theory of liability.' *Journal of Legal Studies* 2, 323-49

– (1974) 'Product liability: the case of an asset with random life.' *American Economic Review* 64, 149-61

Burton, J.F., jr and M. Berkowitz (1971) 'Objectives other than income maintenance for workmen's compensation.' *Journal of Risk and Insurance* 38, 343-55

CCH Canadian (1978) *Employee Benefits and Pension Guide* (Don Mills: CCH Canadian)

Canada (1974) Statistics Canada *Life Tables: Canada and Provinces 1970-72*

Calabresi, G. (1970) *The Costs of Accidents* (New Haven: Yale University Press)

Caldwell, D.D. (1977) 'No fault automobile insurance: an evaluative survey.' *Rutgers Law Review* 30, 909-90

Canada (1966) Report of the Royal Commission on Taxation 3, Part A, *Taxation of Individuals and Families*

– (1978) *Andrews v. Grand & Toy (Alberta) Ltd.*, [1978] 2 S.C.R. 229, 83 D.L.R. (3d) 452; *Thornton v. Board of School Trustees of School District No. 57 (Prince George)*, [1978] 2 S.C.R. 267, 83 D.L.R. (3d) 480; *Arnold v. Teno*, [1978] 2 S.C.R. 287, 83 D.L.R. (3d) 609; *Keizer v. Hanna*, [1978] 2 S.C.R. 342, 82 D.L.R. (3d) 444.

Charles, W.H. (1977) 'Justice in personal injury awards:' in L. Klar, ed., *Studies in Canadian Tort Law* 37-99 (Toronto: Butterworths)

Chelius, J.R. (1973) 'An empirical analysis of safety regulations.' in US National Commission on State Workmen's Compensation Laws *Supplemental Studies* 3, 53-66

– (1976) 'Liability for industrial accidents: a comparison of negligence and strict liability systems.' *Journal of Legal Studies* 5, 293-309

– (1977) *Workplace, Safety and Health: The Role of Worker's Compensation* (Washington DC: American Enterprise Institute for Public Policy Research)

Colantoni, C.S., O.A. Davis, and M. Swaminuthan (1976) 'Imperfect consumers and welfare comparisons of policies concerning information and regulation.' *Bell Journal of Economics* 7, 602-15

Conley, B.C. (1976) 'The value of human life in the demand for safety.' *American Economic Review* 66, 45-55

Conrad, A.F. (1964) *Automobile Accident Costs and Payments: Studies in the Economics of Injury Reparation* (Ann Arbor: University of Michigan Press)

Cook, P.J. (1978 'The value of human life in the demand for safety: comment.' *American Economic Review* 68, 710-11

Cook, P.J. and D.A. Graham (1977) 'The demand for insurance and protection: the case of irreplaceable commodities.' *Quarterly Journal of Economics* XCI, 143-56

Coward, L.E. (1977) *Mercer Handbook of Canadian Pension and Welfare Plans* (Don Mills, Ontario: CCH Canadian Limited)

Diamond, P. (1974) 'Single activity accidents.' *Journal of Legal Studies* 3, 107-62

– (1977), 'Insurance-theoretic aspects of worker's compensation.' In A.S. Blinder and P. Friedman, eds, *Natural Resources, Uncertainty and General Equilibrium Systems* 67-89 (New York: Academic Press)

Diamond, P.A. and J.A. Mirrlees (1975) 'On the assignment of liability: the uniform case.' *Bell Journal of Economics* 6, 487-516

Doudna, D.J. (1977) 'Effect of the economy on group long term disability Claims.' *Journal of Risk and Insurance* 44, 223-35

Duncan, G.J. (1976) 'Earnings functions and nonpecuniary benefits.' *Journal of Human Resources* 11, 463-83

Dunlop, B. (1975) 'No-fault automobile insurance and the negligence action: an expensive anomaly.' *Osgoode Hall Law Journal* 13, 439-47

Ehrlich, I. and G.S. Becker (1972) 'Market insurance, self-insurance, and self-protection.' *Journal of Political Economy* 80, 623-48

Elligett, T. (1979) 'The periodic payment of judgments.' *Insurance Counsel Journal* 46, 130-50

Epple, D. and A. Raviv (1978) 'Product safety: liability rules, market structure, and imperfect information.' *American Economic Review* 68, 80-95

Fleming, J.G. (1969) 'Damages: capital or rent?' *University of Toronto Law Journal* 19, 295-325

– (1977) *The Law of Torts*, 5th ed. (Melbourne: Law Book Co.)

Franklin, M.A. (1975) 'Personal injury in New Zealand and the United States: some striking similarities.' *Stanford Law Review* 27, 653-72

Frech, H.W. III (1976) 'The property rights theory of the firm: empirical results from a natural experiment.' *Journal of Political Economy* 84, 143-52

Fuchs, V.R. (1976) 'From Bismarck to Woodcock: the 'irrational' pursuit of national health insurance.' *Journal of Law and Economics* 11, 347-59

Ghosh, D.A., D. Lees, and W. Seal (1976) *The Economics of Personal Injury* (Westmead, England: Saxon House/Lexington Books)

Glasbeek, H.J. and R.A. Hasson (1977) 'Fault – the great hoax.' In L. Klar, ed., *Studies in Canadian Tort Law* (Toronto: Butterworths) 395-424

Grayston, R.W. (1973) 'Deterrence in automobile liability insurance: the empirical evidence.' *Insurance Counsel Journal* 40, 117-29.

Great Britain (1978) Royal Commission on Civil Liability and Compensation for Personal Injury *Report* 3 volumes

Green, J. (1976) 'On the optimal structure of liability laws.' *Bell Journal of Economics* 7, 553-74

Gregory, P. and M. Gisser (1973) 'Theoretical aspects of workmen's compensation.' In US National Commission on State Workmen's Compensation Laws, *Supplemental Studies* 3, 108-28

Grubel, H.G. (1971) 'Risk, uncertainty and moral hazard.' *Journal of Risk and Insurance* 38, 99-106

Haber, L.D. (1973) 'Social planning for disability.' *Journal of Human Resources* 8, 33-55

Hambor, J.C. (1975) *Unemployment and Disability* (Washington: US Social Security Administration, Staff Paper 20)

Harper, F.V. and F. James (1956) *The Law of Torts* (Boston: Little Brown)

Hasson, R.A. (1976) 'Blood-feuds, writs and rifles: a reply to Professor Linden.' *Osgoode Hall Law Journal* 14, 445-55

Holmström, B. (1979) 'Moral hazard and observability.' *Bell Journal of Economics* 10, 74-91

Ison, T.G. (1967) *The Forensic Lottery* (London: Staples Press)

– (1969) 'Highway accidents and the demise of tort liability.' *Canadian Bar Review* 17, 305-12

Jaynes, G.D. (1978) 'Equilibria in monopolistically competitive insurance markets.' *Journal of Economic Theory* 19, 394-422

Johnson, W.R. (1977) 'Choice of compulsory insurance schemes under adverse selection.' *Public Choice* 31, 23-35

Johnson, W.G. and E.H. Murphy (1975) 'The response of low-income households to income losses from disability.' *Industrial and Labor Relations Review* 29, 85-96

Jones-Lee, M. (1974) 'The value of changes in the probability of death or injury.' *Journal of Political Economy* 82, 835-49

– (1976) *The Value of Life: An Economic Analysis* (Chicago: University of Chicago Press)

Kahneman D. and A. Tversky (1979) "Prospect theory: an analysis of decision under risk.' *Econometrica* 47, 263-91

Kasper, D.M. (1975) 'An alternative to workmen's compensation.' *Industrial and Labor Relations Review* 28, 535-48

Keeley, M.C., P.K. Robins, R.G. Spiegelman, and R.W. West (1978) 'The labor supply effects and costs of alternative negative income tax programs.' *Journal of Human Resources* 13, 3-36

Keeton, R. and J. O'Connell (1965) *Basic Protection for the Traffic Victim: A Blueprint for Reforming Automobile Insurance* (Boston: Little Brown)

Kennedy, K.F. and R.I. Mehr (1977) 'A case study in private vs public enterprise: the Manitoba experience with automobile insurance.' *Journal of Risk and Insurance* 44, 595-621

Knoeber, C.R. (1976) 'Legal penalties and compensation for auto accidents.' Unpublished Ph D dissertation (University of California, Los Angeles)

Kunreuther, H. et al. (1978) *Disaster Insurance Protection* (New York: John Wiley & Sons)

Lando, M.E. and A. Krute (1976) 'Disability insurance: program issues and research.' *Social Security Bulletin* 39, 3-17

Lees, D. and N. Doherty (1973) 'Compensation for personal injury.' *Lloyd's Bank Review* 108, 18-32

Legge B.J. (1972) *The Canadian System of Workmen's Compensation* (Toronto: Workmen's Compensation Board)

Lichtenstein, S., P. Slovic, B. Fischhoff, M. Layman, and B. Combs (1978) 'Judged frequency of lethal events.' *Journal of Experimental Psychology: Human Learning and Memory* 4, 551-78

Linden A.M. (1965) *Report of the Osgoode Hall Study on Compensation for Victims of Automobile Accidents* (Toronto: Ryerson Press)

– (1975) 'Faulty no-fault: a critique of the Ontario Law Reform Commission Report on motor vehicle accident compensation.' *Osgoode Hall Law Journal* 13, 449-60

– (1977) *Canadian Tort Law* (Toronto: Butterworths)

Lucas, R.E.B. (1972) 'Working conditions, wage-rates and human capital: a hedonic study.' Unpublished Ph D dissertation (Massachusetts Institute of Technology)

Luft, H.S. (1975) 'The impact of poor health on earnings.' *Review of Economics and Statistics* 57, 43-57

McKean, R.N. (1970) 'Products liability: implications of some changing property rights.' *Quarterly Journal of Economics* 84, 611-26

McLure, C.E. (1977) 'The incidence of the financing of unemployment insurance.' *Industrial and Labor Relations Review* 30, 469-79

Manitoba (1977) *Accident and Sickness Compensation in Manitoba*

Marshall, J.M. (1976) 'Moral hazard.' *American Economic Review* 66, 880-90

Miller, J.H. (1978) 'Disability insurance: an assessment of its social value.' *CLU Journal* 32, 12-24

Mishan, E.J. (1971) 'Evaluation of life and limb: a theoretical approach.' *Journal of Political Economy* 79, 687-705

Morgan, J.N. et al. (1959) *Lump Sum Redemption Settlement and Rehabilitation* (Ann Arbor: University of Michigan Survey Research Center)

Morris, C. (1975) 'Annuities to settle cases.' Panel discussion, *Insurance Counsel Journal* 42, 367-85 (Morris's contribution on 374 especially)

Mossin, J. (1968) 'Aspects of rational insurance purchasing.' *Journal of Political Economy* 76, 553-68

Murray, M.L. (1971) 'A deductible selection model: development and application.' *Journal of Risk and Insurance* 38, 423-36

– (1972) 'Empirical utility functions and insurance consumption decisions.' *Journal of Risk and Insurance* 39, 31-41

Musgrave, R.A. (1968) 'The role of social insurance in an overall program.' In W.G. Bowen, F.H. Harbison, R.A. Lester, and H.M. Somers, eds, *Princeton Symposium on the American System of Social Insurance* 23-40 (New York: McGraw-Hill)

Nagi, S.Z. (1969) *Disability and Rehabilitation* (Columbus: Ohio State University Press)

Nagi, S.Z. and L.W. Hadley (1972) 'Disability behavior: income change and motivation to work.' *Industrial and Labor Relations Review* 25, 223-33

Needleman, L. (1979) 'The value of changes in the risk of death by those at risk.' Waterloo Economic Series no. 103, University of Waterloo

Neter, J. et al. (1968) 'Comparison of independent and joint decision-making for two insurance decisions.' *Journal of Risk and Insurance* 35, 87-105

Neter, J. and C.A. Williams jr (1971) 'Acceptability of three normative methods of insurance decision making.' *Journal of Risk and Insurance* 38, 385-408

New Zealand (1967) Report of the Royal Commission of Inquiry, *Compensation for Personal Injury in New Zealand*

– (1972) Report of the Royal Commission of Inquiry, *Social Security in New Zealand*

Nichols, A.L. and R. Zeckhauser (1977) 'Government comes to the workplace: an assessment of OSHA.' *The Public Interest* 49, 39-69

O'Connell, J. (1975) *Ending Insult to Injury: No-Fault Insurance for Products and Services* (Champaign, Ill.: University of Illinois Press)

– (1977) 'Operation of no-fault auto laws: a survey of the surveys.' *Nebraska Law Review* 56, 23-50

Oi, W.Y. (1973a) 'Workmen's compensation and industrial safety.' In US National Commission on State Workmen's Compensation Laws, *Supplemental Studies* 1, 42-107

- (1973b) 'The economics of product safety.' *Bell Journal of Economics and Management Science* 4, 3-28
Ontario (1973a) *Report of the Task Force: The Administration of Workmen's Compensation in Ontario*
- (1973b) Ontario Law Reform Commission *Report on Motor Vehicle Accident Compensation* (Toronto: Ministry of the Attorney General)
- (1976) Ministry of Labour, Research Branch, 'Sick leave and weekly sickness and accident indemnity insurance plans in Ontario collective agreements.'
Ontario (1977a) Select Committee on Company Law, *The Insurance Industry: First Report on Automobile Industry*
- (1977b) Advisory Council on the Physically Handicapped, 'Income maintenance for the physically handicapped'
- (1978) Select Committee on Company Law, *The Insurance Industry: Second Report on Automobile Insurance*
Palmer, G.W.R. (1977) 'Accident prevention in New Zealand: the first two years.' *American Journal of Comparative Law* 25, 1-45
Parkin, J.M. and S.Y. Wu (1972) 'Choice involving unwanted risky events and optimal insurance.' *American Economic Review* 62, 982-7
Pay Research Bureau (1977) *Employee Benefits and Conditions of Employment in Canada* (Ottawa: Public Service Staff Relations Board)
Pauly, M.V. (1970) 'The welfare economics of community rating.' *Journal of Risk and Insurance* 37, 407-18
- (1974) 'Overinsurance and public provision of insurance: the roles of moral hazard and adverse selection.' *Quarterly Journal of Economics* 88, 44-62
Peltzman, S. (1975) 'The effects of automobile safety regulation.' *Journal of Political Economy* 83, 677-725
Pesando, J.E. (1979) *Private Pension Plans in an Inflationary Climate: Limitations and Policy Alternatives* (Ottawa: Economic Council of Canada)
Pesando, J.E. and S.A. Rea jr (1977) *Public and Private Pensions in Canada* (Toronto: University of Toronto Press for the Ontario Economic Council)
Posner, R.A. (1977) *Economic Analysis of Law* (Boston: Little, Brown)
Quirin, G.D., P.J. Halpern, B.A. Kalymon, G.F. Mathewson, and W.R. Waters (1974) *Competition, Economic Efficiency and Profitability in the Canadian Property and Casualty Insurance Industry* (Toronto: Insurance Bureau of Canada)
Raviv, R. (1979) 'The design of an optimal insurance policy.' *American Economic Review* 69, 84-96
Rawls, J. (1971) *A Theory of Justice* (Cambridge: Harvard University Press)
Rea, S.A. (1974) 'Incentive effects of alternative negative income tax plans.' *Journal of Public Economics* 3, 237-49

- (1979) 'Stabilization of lifetime consumption in a world of uncertain inflation: implications for annuity design.' Unpublished ms.
- (1981) 'Workmen's compensation and occupational safety under imperfect information.' *American Economic Review* 70, 80-93

Riley, J.G. (1979) 'Noncooperative equilibrium and market signalling.' *American Economic Review* 69, 303-7

Rosen, S. (1974) 'Hedonic prices and implicit markets: product differentiation in pure competition.' *Journal of Political Economy* 82, 34-55

Rothschild, M. and J. Stiglitz (1976) 'Equilibrium in competitive insurance markets: an essay on the economics of imperfect information.' *Quarterly Journal of Economics* 90, 629-49

Roumasset, J.A. (1976) *Rice and Risk* (Amsterdam: North Holland)

Russell, L.B. (1973) 'Pricing industrial accidents.' In US National Commission on State Workmen's Compensation Laws, *Supplemental Studies* 3, 27-52
- (1974) 'Safety incentives in workmen's compensation insurance.' *Journal of Human Resources* 9, 361-75

Saskatchewan (1976) *Report of the Sickness and Accident Insurance Committee*

Scheffler, R.M. and G. Iden (1974) 'The effect of disability on labor supply.' *Industrial and Labor Relations Review* 28, 122-232

Schelling, T.C. (1978) 'Egonomics, or the art of self-management.' *American Economic Review* 68, 290-4

Schwartz, G.T. (1978) 'Contributory and comparative negligence: a reappraisal.' *The Yale Law Journal* 87, 697-727

Scott, L.K. (1973) 'The end of a faulted system: New Zealand adopts a no-fault approach to personal injury compensation.' *Law and the Social Order* 679-705

Shavell, S. (1979) 'On moral hazard and insurance.' *Quarterly Journal of Economics* 93, 541-62

Sheshinski, E. (1977) 'Adverse selection and optimum insurance policies.' In A.S. Blinder and P. Friedman, eds, *Natural Resources Uncertainty and General Equilibrium Systems* (New York: Academic Press)

Simkins, J. and V. Tickner (1978) *Whose Benefit?* (London: The Economist Intelligence Unit Ltd)

Smith, A. ([1776] 1937) *The Wealth of Nations* (New York: Modern Library)

Smith, R.S. (1973) 'An analysis of work injuries in manufacturing industry.' In US National Commission on State Workmen's Compensation Laws, *Supplemental Studies* 3, 9-26
- (1976) *The Occupational Safety and Health Act* (Washington, DC: American Enterprise Institute for Public Policy Research)

- (1979) "Compensating wage differentials and public policy: a review.' *Industrial and Labor Relations Review* 32, 339-52
Smith, V.L. (1968) 'Optimal insurance coverage.' *Journal of Political Economy* 76 68-77
Spence, Michael (1977) 'Consumer misperceptions, product failure and producer liability.' *Review of Economic Studies* 44, 561-72
Spence, M. and R. Zeckhauser (1971) 'Insurance, information and individual action.' *American Economic Review* 61, 380-7
Steele, G.R. (1974) 'Industrial accidents: an economic interpretation.' *Applied Economics* 6, 143-55
Stiglitz, J.E. (1977) 'Monopoly, non-linear pricing and imperfect information: the insurance market.' *Review of Economic Studies* 44, 407-30
Thaler, R. (1974) 'The value of saving a life: a market estimate.' Unpublished Ph D dissertation (University of Rochester)
Thaler, R. and S. Rosen (1975) 'The value of saving a life: evidence from the labor market.' In N.E. Terleckyj, ed., *Household Production and Consumption* (New York: National Bureau of Economic Research) 265-98
Tversky, A. and D. Kahneman (1974) 'Judgment under uncertainty: heuristics and biases.' *Science* 185, 1124-31
United States (1972a) *Report of the National Commission on State Workmen's Compensation Laws*
- (1972b) *Supplemental Studies for the National Commission on State Workmen's Compensation Laws*
- (1976) House Committee on Ways and Means, Subcommittee on Social Security, *Disability Insurance* Legislative Issue Paper
- (1977) Department of Transportation, *State No-Fault Automobile Insurance Experience* 1971-7
Van de Water, P.N. (1979) 'Disability insurance.' *American Economic Review* 69, 275-8
Vennell, M.A. (1975) 'The scope of the national no-fault accident compensation in Australia and New Zealand.' *Australian Law Journal* 49, 22-9
Viscusi, W.K. (1978) Wealth effects and earnings premiums for job hazards.' *Review of Economics and Statistics* 60, 408-16
- (1979) 'Job hazards and worker quit rates: an analysis of adaptive worker behavior.' *International Economic Review* 20, 29-58
Widiss, A.I., R.R. Bovbjerg, D.F. Cavers, J.W. Little, R.S. Clark, G.E. Waterson, and T.C. Jones (1977) *No-Fault Automobile Insurance in Action: The Experiences in Massachusetts, Florida, Delaware and Michigan* (Dobbs Ferry, NY: Oceana Publications, Inc.)

Williams, C.A., jr (1966) "Attitudes toward speculative risks as an indication of attitudes toward pure risks.' *Journal of Risk and Insurance* 33, 577-86

Williamson, O., D.G. Olson, and A. Ralston (1967) 'Externalities, insurance, and disability analysis.' *Economica* NS 34, 235-53

Wilson, C. (1977) 'A model of insurance markets with incomplete information.' *Journal of Economic Theory* 16, 167-207

Wittman, D. (1977) 'Prior regulation versus post liability: the choice between input and output monitoring.' *Journal of Legal Studies* 6, 193-212

Wyatt Company (1978) *Examination of the Financial Structure of the Workmen's Compensation Board and an Assessment of the Actuarial Deficit*. Report submitted to Ontario Ministry of Labour (Toronto)

Zeckhauser, R. (1970) 'Medical insurance: a case study of the tradeoff between risk spreading and appropriate incentives.' *Journal of Economic Theory* 2, 10-16

– (1973) 'Coverage for catastrophic illness.' *Public Policy* 21, 149-72

www.ingramcontent.com/pod-product-compliance
Lightning Source LLC
Chambersburg PA
CBHW020257030426
42336CB00010B/806